T0345279

PYTHON

Python's simplicity and versatility make it an ideal language for both beginners and experienced programmers. Its syntax facilitates a smooth learning curve, enabling individuals to concentrate on grasping programming concepts instead of wrestling with intricate syntax rules. The extensive standard library reinforces its practicality, offering pre-built modules and functions that reduce manual coding efforts. Python's versatility is evident in its applications, spanning web development, data analysis, Machine Learning and automation.

The language's interactive nature supports real-time code experimentation, stepping up the learning process and enhancing understanding. Python's wealth of online resources further enriches the learning experience, fostering a community where individuals can develop their programming skills.

Python: A Practical Learning Approach exemplifies Python's simplicity and versatility with numerous examples, ensuring a seamless learning journey. Beyond theory, the language's practicality allows learners to actively apply their knowledge in real-world scenarios, establishing Python as an asset in education.

PYTHON

A Practical Learning Approach

T.S. Murugesh
Shriram K. Vasudevan
Sini Raj Pulari

CRC Press
Taylor & Francis Group
Boca Raton London New York

CRC Press is an imprint of the
Taylor & Francis Group, an **informa** business

Designed cover image: © Shutterstock

First edition published 2025
by CRC Press
2385 NW Executive Center Drive, Suite 320, Boca Raton FL 33431

and by CRC Press
4 Park Square, Milton Park, Abingdon, Oxon, OX14 4RN

CRC Press is an imprint of Taylor & Francis Group, LLC

© 2025 T.S. Murugesh, Shriram K. Vasudevan, and Sini Raj Pulari

Library of Congress Cataloging-in-Publication Data
Names: Murugesh, T. S., author. | Vasudevan, Shriram K., author. | Pulari,
Sini Raj, author.
Title: Python : a practical learning approach / T. S. Murugesh, Shriram K. Vasudevan,
and Sini Raj Pulari.
Description: First edition. | Boca Raton : CRC Press, 2025. |
Includes bibliographical references and index.
Identifiers: LCCN 2024006616 (print) | LCCN 2024006617 (ebook) |
ISBN 9781032712642 (hbk) | ISBN 9781032712666 (pbk) | ISBN 9781032712673 (ebk)
Subjects: LCSH: Python (Computer program language)
Classification: LCC QA76.73.P98 M87 2025 (print) |
LCC QA76.73.P98 (ebook) | DDC 005.13/3--dc23/eng/20240422
LC record available at https://lccn.loc.gov/2024006616
LC ebook record available at https://lccn.loc.gov/2024006617

ISBN: 978-1-032-71264-2 (hbk)
ISBN: 978-1-032-71266-6 (pbk)
ISBN: 978-1-032-71267-3 (ebk)

DOI: 10.1201/9781032712673

Typeset in Caslon
by SPi Technologies India Pvt Ltd (Straive)

Contents

Preface

Python, acknowledged for its simplicity and versatility, is particularly conducive to a practical learning approach, making it an ideal language for beginners and seasoned programmers alike. Its readability and concise syntax facilitate a smoother learning curve, allowing individuals to focus on understanding programming concepts rather than struggling with complex syntax rules. Python's extensive standard library further reinforces its practicality by providing a wealth of pre-built modules and functions, reducing the need for manual coding, and enabling developers to achieve more with fewer lines of code. This practicality is evident in Python's applicability across diverse domains, from web development and data analysis to Machine Learning and automation.

Python's interactive nature allows learners to experiment with code in real time, reinforcing their understanding of concepts. This approach not only accelerates the learning process but also fosters a deeper and more intuitive comprehension of programming principles. Moreover, Python's vast online resources enhance the overall learning experience, creating an environment where individuals can grow and develop their programming skills.

Python: A Practical Learning Approach is characterized by the simplicity, versatility, and positioning of Python as an exemplary language for those seeking to enter the world of programming or expand their skillset. The book presents a plethora of examples to provide a seamless learning experience. The language's practicality extends beyond mere theoretical understanding, allowing learners to actively apply their knowledge to real-world scenarios, making Python an asset in the educational landscape. Readers can reach out to the authors with any constructive criticisms.

About the Authors

Dr. T. S. Murugesh has nearly 24 years' experience in academia in the fields of Analog and Digital Electronics, Automation and Control, IoT, System Design, Image Processing, Artificial Intelligence, Machine Learning, Instrumentation and Computational Bioengineering. After a tenure of almost 19 years with the Department of Electronics and Instrumentation Engineering, Faculty of Engineering and Technology, Annamalai University, Tamil Nadu, India, he is currently working as Associate Professor in the Department of Electronics and Communication Engineering, Government College of Engineering Srirangam, Tiruchirappalli, Tamil Nadu, India. He has delivered several talks at international-level conferences of high repute and has given over two dozen invited lectures at the national level in various institutions, including Sastra University, Annamalai University, Mahatma Gandhi University, Kerala, National Institute of Technology, Tiruchirappalli, and others. He has around 50 peer-reviewed indexed papers in journals, including Springer, Springer Nature, Elsevier, Wiley, Inderscience, etc. He has organized several Faculty Development Programmes at the national level, and is a reviewer for *IEEE*, *Inderscience* and many other peer-reviewed journals. He has coauthored five books for CRC Press Taylor & Francis Group (UK) and is currently co-authoring one book for Nova Science Publishers, USA and two further books for CRC Press.

He has assumed the role of Mentor, Primary Evaluator for the Government of India's Smart India Hackathon 2022, Toycathon2021, a Judge in the Grand Finale in "Toycathon 2021", an evaluator in "The Kavach2023" Cybersecurity Hackathon, organized by the Ministry of Home Affairs (MHA) in collaboration with the Ministry of Education's (MoE) Innovation Cell, Government of India. He is a hackathon enthusiast, and his team has won First Prize in the CloudFest Hackathon 2 presented by Google Cloud, DigitalGov Hack, the Hackathon by WSIS Forum 2023 and Digital Government Authority, Saudi Arabia. His team has also won the MSME Idea Hackathon 2.0 and received 15 Lakhs funding from MSME (Ministry of Micro, Small and Medium Enterprises) Innovative Scheme, Government of India as well as the Second Prize in the IFG x TA Hub Hackathon 2022.

Murugesh is a certified Intel oneAPI Innovator, a Mentor under the "National Initiative for Technical Teachers Training" program from AICTE, and the National Institute of Technical Teachers Training and Research, and a Certified Microsoft Educator Academy Professional. He is also a Master Assessor for a Naan Mudhalvan Program, 2023, devised by the Government of Tamil Nadu, and a reviewer of B.E./B. Tech Technical Books in the Regional Language scheme of AICTE, coordinated by the Centre for Development of Tamil in Engineering and Technology, Anna University, Tamil Nadu, India. Huawei has recognized him for academic collaboration. He is a Conference Committee Member and Publishing Committee Member of the International Association of Applied Science and Technology. He is also a member of the Editorial Board of the *American Journal of Embedded Systems and Applications*. He has also served as Technical Program Committee member for a Springer-sponsored, Scopus-Indexed International Conference conducted at Sharda University, India and a Scientific Committee Member for an international conference conducted at the Sultanate of Oman, as well as a chairperson in an International Hybrid Conference at Mahatma Gandhi University Kerala, India. He has held various academic responsibilities such as chairman for Anna University Central Valuation, Chief Superintendent for the Anna University Theory Examinations and he is presently the Exam Cell Coordinator for his institution. He also holds professional body membership within the Institution of Engineers (India).

Dr. Shriram K. Vasudevan has over 17 years' combined experience in industry and academia. He holds a Doctorate in Embedded Systems. He has authored/co-authored 45 books for various publishers, including Taylor & Francis, Oxford University Press, and Wiley. He also has been granted 13 patents to date. Shriram is a hackathon enthusiast and has received awards from Harvard University, AICITE, CII, Google, TDRA Dubai, the Government of Saudi Arabia, the Government of India and many more. He has published more than 150 research articles. He was associated with L&T Technology Services before taking up his current role with Intel. Shriram Vasudevan runs a YouTube channel in his name, which has more than 43K subscribers and maintains a wide range of playlists on varied topics. Dr. Shriram is also a public speaker. He is Intel one API-certified Instructor, a Google Cloud Ambassador, a Streamlit Education Ambassador, an AWS Ambassador, an ACM Distinguished Speaker and a NASSCOM Prime Ambassador. Shriram is a Fellow of the IEI, a Fellow of the IETE and a Senior Member of the IEEE.

Ms. Sini Raj Pulari, professor and tutor, is presently with Government University (Bahrain Polytechnic, Faculty of EDICT) in The Kingdom of Bahrain. She has 16 years of experience in various reputed Indian universities and industries by contributing to the teaching field and carrying out activities to maintain and develop research and professional activities relevant to Computer Science Engineering. Her research interests include Natural Language Processing, Recommender Systems, Information Retrieval, Deep Learning and Machine Learning. She has authored 20+ Scopus-indexed publications and co-authored *Deep Learning: A Comprehensive Guide* (CRC Press/Taylor & Francis). Sini has developed and guided around 40+ undergraduate and postgraduate projects and is an active member on the boards of curriculum development for various universities. She has delivered 40+ invited lectures on the applications and emerging trends in a variety of upcoming technological and research advancements. She was a speaker at the workshops "AI for ALL" and "Understanding Deep Learning Algorithm – Convolution Neural Networks with Real Time Applications, using Python, Keras and Tensor Flow". Sini has also participated in the MENA Hackathon group discussion on the topic "Innovating tech-based solutions for challenges in the healthcare and energy, environment & sustainability sectors", which was in partnership with Tamkeen, powered by Amazon Web Services (AWS) and Elijah Coaching and Consulting Services. She has completed various reputed certifications such as Apple Certified Trainer, SCJP, Oracle Certified Associate, and APQMR-Quality Matters.

1

THE INTRODUCTORY
DISCUSSION

LEARNING OBJECTIVES

After reading this chapter, readers will have learned the following:

- What Python is
- Why Python is so popular
- Installation guidelines
- Hello, world with Python
- Execution options
- Numbers and variables
- Data types
- Some interesting quiz questions.

1.1 Introduction

Let us start with a question: why should someone learn Python in the first place? Then we can move on to learn the technical things and allied contents.

In recent years, Python has been growing tremendously and there is a lot of attention being paid to it. Why is this happening? Why are there a lot of takers for Python? We need to understand that first before moving along the learning curve.

The reasons are listed one after another as follows:

a. **Ease of learning** – It is the very important reason to be discussed. Python is simple and easy to use. It is very easy to understand a Python code and there is no complexity involved. Reading a Python code is as good as reading English documents. Even if you have no prior programming experience or learning, you can learn Python with ease.

b. **Open Source** – Python is open source, and this is one of the very important reasons for its rapid growth and usage. There is no fee involved in using Python and the amount of resources available for Python make this a really cool language to learn.

c. **Versatility** – Python is widely regarded as being super versatile. Yes, Python can be used for building a variety of applications catering to different domains/sectors. One can build Machine Learning (ML), Deep Learning (DL), Natural Language Processing (NLP), Data Analysis, Big Data, Automation, Embedded Applications and many other applications with Python. Therefore, it is an ideal choice for anyone to learn.

d. **Community presence** – These days community presence is very important for any language or a tool to grow and to find a large user base. Python is excellently supported by massive and active developers. There are so many resources one could find for Python online. Multiple channels teach Python. Solving problems which may arise when you use Python can be sorted with ease with the kind of support we have for this language.

e. **Jobs and the market** – Python has been one of the most wanted skillsets in the recent past. In addition, the versatility that it brings to the table makes it most chosen by the developers and also across the industry.

f. **Cross-platform support and compatibility** – Python is available for all the known operating systems and platforms we are aware of. It suits well for Windows, Linux and macOS. Hence, it is highly preferred by the developers.

g. **Evolution of Machine Learning and Artificial Intelligence (AI)** – After the recent humongous growth in the field of Artificial Intelligence (AI), Python has become even more popular. Many libraries, like NumPy, SciPy, Scikit Learn, TensorFlow, Pytorch and more, make Python the most desirable language. It is easier to develop AI applications with Python than other programming languages.

h. **Scalability** – Python is most suitable for small-scale, medium-scale and large-scale applications. Therefore, this is also an important aspect of why someone has to learn Python.

Considering all the above facts, one can learn Python and it is definitely a good move for the learner. Learning Python is a good investment for a bright future.

Now, having understood the benefits of learning Python, we can learn the definition of Python. Can we?

1.2 What is Python?

Python, as we have seen in the previous section, is a programming language. It is a general-purpose programming language that is very easy to learn and use. It is also regarded as an interpreted and high-level programming language, which offers the users a lot of flexibility and versatility. Python, which was created by Guido van Rossum and first released in 1991, has been growing consistently and is now one of the most used programming languages across the globe.

The next question, which the readers might pose, is: why is Python called an interpreted language? The answer is simple: it uses the interpreter to execute the code. The interpreter reads the program, and translates the same line by line to machine code. It ca then be executed. Make a note of the point, it happens line by line.

A simple workflow of how a typical Python file is executed is presented below:

1. First, one should write the code and save the file as a .py file. It indicates the file has Python code. This file shall be human-readable, and is typically called a high-level language.
2. The interpreter is called now, which is responsible for reading the code and executing the same.
3. Code parsing happens next, in which the interpreter reads the code line by line. Each line shall be interpreted, and it will be translated to a form that the computer can understand. Here, the human-readable format to machine-readable format translation happens, that too on the fly.
4. The interpreter then executes the code, one line at a time.

Since the Python code is directly executed by the interpreter, there is no compilation step required as needed in the C or C++ which you must have come across. Compilers need the code to be compiled and then executed. This is a major difference to be understood.

The interpreted nature carries its own benefits and drawbacks. The advantage is it is very easy to develop, and no platform dependency challenges are faced. The Python code can run on different machines without any modifications needed. On the other side, Python handles the code line by line. Hence, it is slower than the way the compilers handle the code.

1.3 Let's Write Our First Python Code

As we know, learning starts with "How do we run the Python programs?" It is easy. Yes, it really is.

First, one must download Python. It is harmless, and easy to download and install too. Visit www.python.org to get the executables for your machine. One can download the latest version of Python as per the requirement. One can pick any version and it is suggested that the readers should opt for the latest version. One can download Python for Windows or Mac. When it comes to Linux, Python is mostly pre-installed and if there is a requirement for an upgrade, it can easily be done.

One can see the Python landing page, as shown below in Figure 1.1. One can also see the recent version of the Python available for download is 3.11.5.

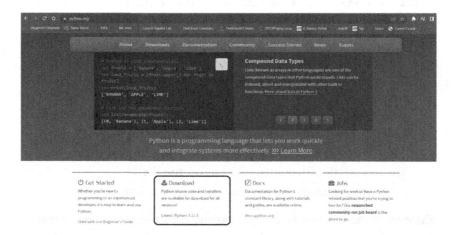

Figure 1.1 python.org – The landing page.

On clicking the download button, as shown in Figure 1.1, one would get the options for the installer download as shown in Figure 1.2. The user must carefully choose the installer, based on the OS and the 32/64 bit variant. It will take a few seconds for the download to be completed.

Figure 1.2 python.org – Installation options.

We have used Windows Installer (64-bit) and on clicking the hyperlink, the installer is downloaded as shown in Figure 1.3.

Figure 1.3 The installer.

If the users have already installed some old versions of Python, this installer will upgrade the version. It may take a few minutes for the installation to be completed. One can see the progress of the installation as shown in Figure 1.4.

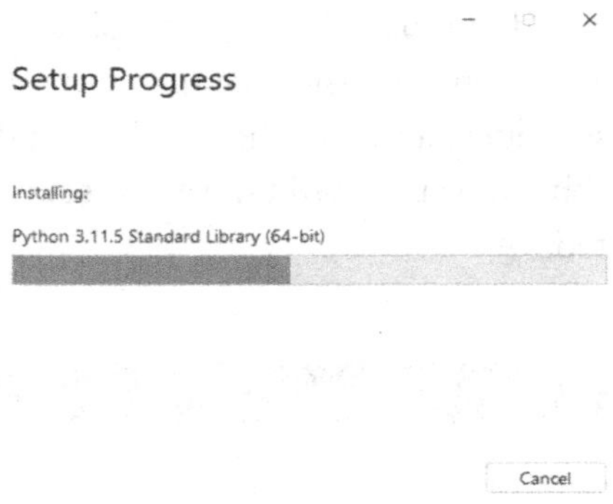

Setup Progress

Installing:

Python 3.11.5 Standard Library (64-bit)

Cancel

Figure 1.4 Python installation progress – Windows.

The installation shall be completed, and one can see the message on the screen. That's it. Python is installed and you can start the learning. One can confirm if the installation has happened correctly by typing Python in the start menu of Windows as shown below in Figure 1.5. This will show the icon of Python and clicking on it will enable you to launch Python.

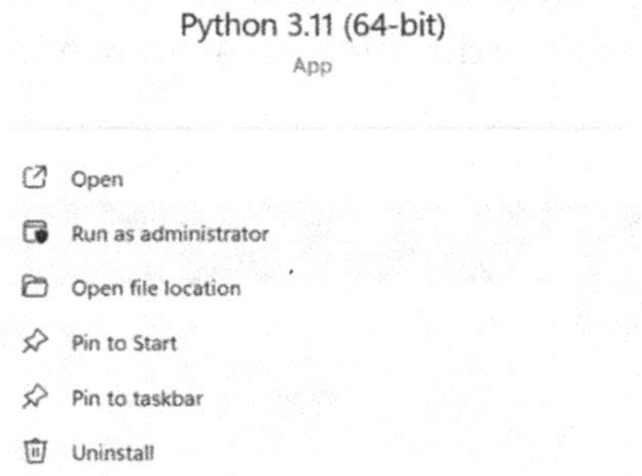

Python 3.11 (64-bit)
App

☐ Open
⊡ Run as administrator
🗁 Open file location
⇗ Pin to Start
⇗ Pin to taskbar
🗑 Uninstall

Figure 1.5 Installation complete.

The readers are strongly recommended to visit https://www.python. org/about/ to understand more about the Python, the community initiatives, the Open-Source nature of Python and gain access to a lot of learning resources. One can see the screenshot of the https://www. python.org/about/ as presented in Figure 1.6.

Figure 1.6 Learn from the 'About' page.

Welcome to the world of Python! It's interesting and rewarding too. Can we get our first Python code up and running?

First, learn how to create a Python file? Open an editor (Something like a notepad ++ or notepad). Type the instructions (the code, yes, which could be for adding two numbers). Save the file with filename. py as the extension. Run the file with the interpreter, and one can get the output, immediately. One can see the code typed and saved as 1.py, as shown in Figure 1.7. This code will simply print Hello, World! We shall discuss more on the coding a little later.

```
1.py - C:/Users/shriramk/OneDrive - Intel Corporation/Desktop/PythonBook/1.py (3.11.5)
File  Edit  Format  Run  Options  Window  Help
# This program prints Hello, world!
print('Hello, world!')
```

Figure 1.7 Printing Hello, world!

The Figures 1.8 and 1.9 offers a glimpse of the steps to run the first code and to get the relevant output respectively.

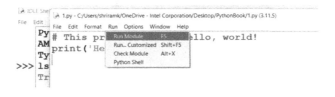

Figure 1.8 Running the first Python code.

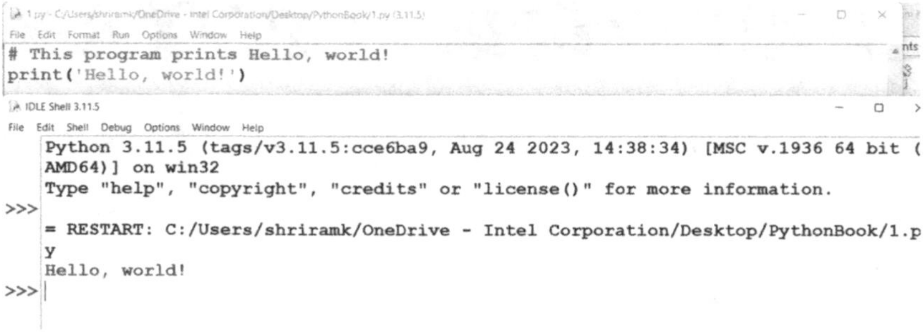

Figure 1.9 The output.

If the user is not interested in the graphical user interface (GUI) way of doing it, a command prompt can always be used. One can refer to Figure 1.10 to understand the same.

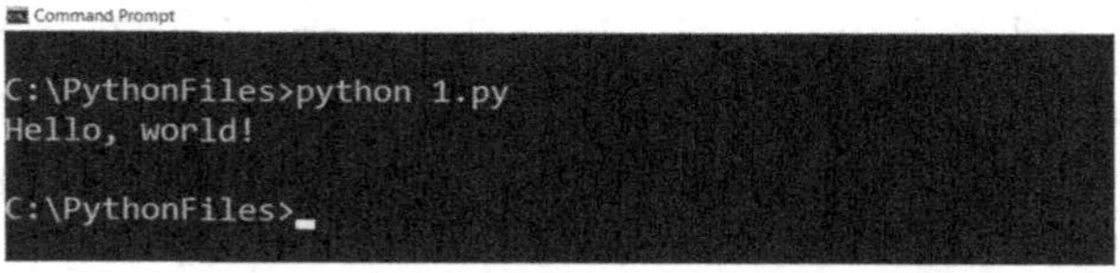

Figure 1.10 The command prompt way of execution.

In Unix/Linux – use chmod 777 filename.py to compile the code and./filename.py to run the code. (Or, simple, use python filename.py.)

There is a catch. If the user does not want to execute the instructions by storing them into a Python file, is there an option? Yes, there is an option. One can refer to Figure 1.11 to understand the way it is done through the IDLE Shell directly.

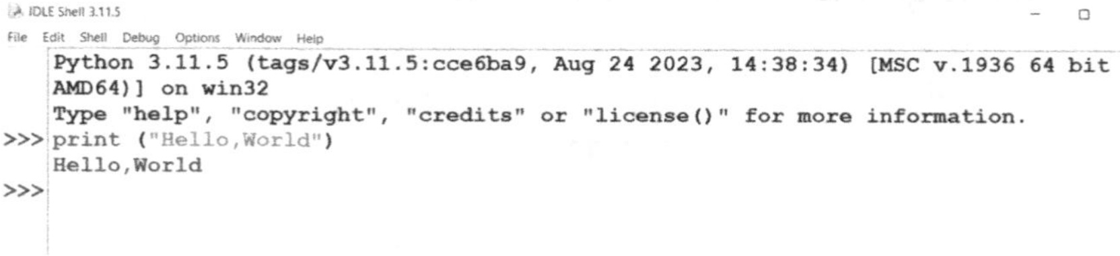

Figure 1.11 The Shell way.

To come out of the shell, one should type exit(). The above method may not be so handy if you have many lines for execution.

Yes, take a deep breath. The first file is executed.

1.4 Learn the Fundamentals – With the Numbers

Python is very easy to learn and use. Spaces between the numbers and operators are not mandatory! It is for enhanced readability and nothing else. One can have a look at Figure 1.12 to understand the point conveyed.

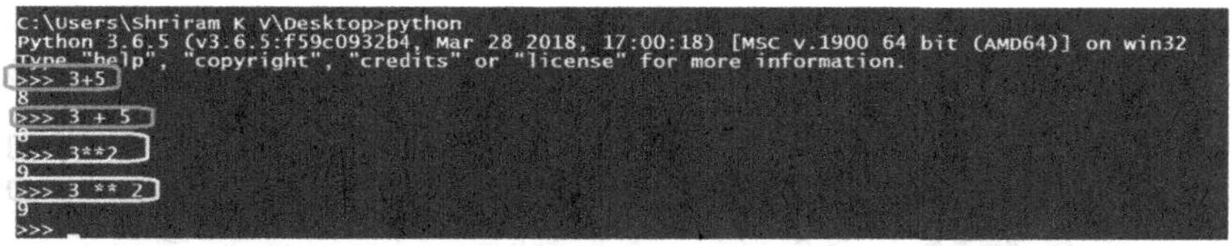

Figure 1.12 Numbers and spacing.

As a next step, Let's try dividing a number by zero. (This is interesting.) Have you heard of the divide by zero error! Here you go. 10 when divided by 2 is correct and the results appear in front. But, when 10 is divided by 0, it is an error. Zero division error shall be presented, and this is to be known. One can refer to Figure 1.13 for the same.

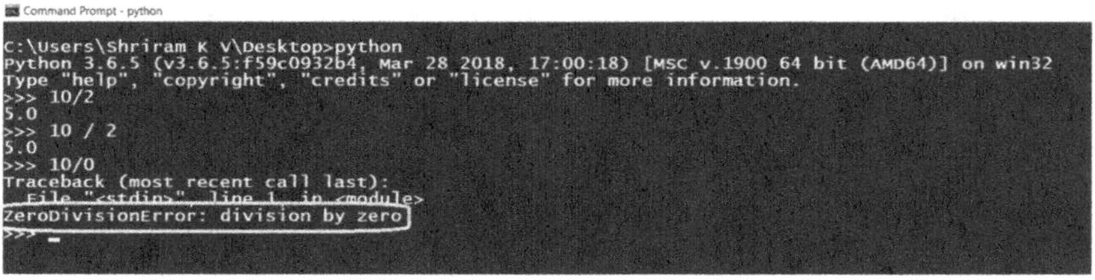

Figure 1.13 Divide by zero.

It is time to do simple multiplication and addition. One can see the multiplication and division examples presented as in Figure 1.14.

Let us go ahead and do division again but this time with quotient and remainder. One should use // to get the quotient and % to get the remainder. Also, one should note that this works fine with both int and float types (Figure 1.15).

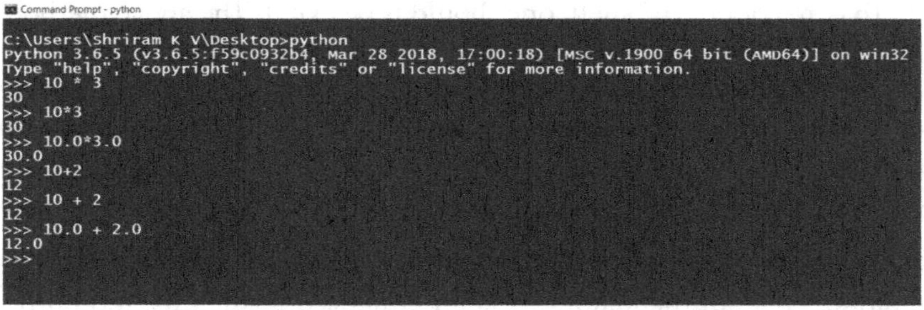

Figure 1.14　Multiplication and addition examples.

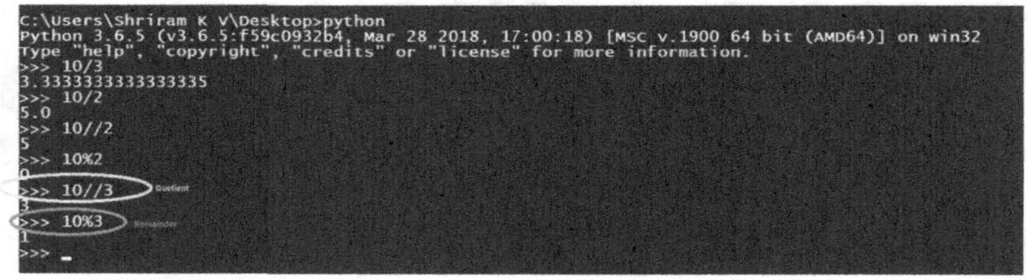

Figure 1.15　Division with quotient and remainder.

Can we learn the variables now? Yes, it is very important for anyone to learn this. It is all automatic here. This means that the memory allocation happens as soon as a value is assigned to a variable.

- *Name of the variable = value to be stored in the variable.*

An example is handy as always and is presented as in Figure 1.16. The code now has value assigned with an integer, followed by miles assigned with float and name with a string. This is the beauty of Python; it is automatic, you need not specify what the data type is. The output for the code shown in Figure 1.16 is presented as in Figure 1.17.

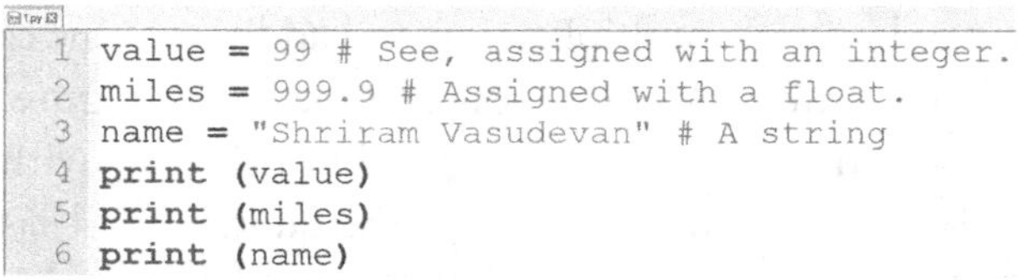

```
1  value = 99 # See, assigned with an integer.
2  miles = 999.9 # Assigned with a float.
3  name = "Shriram Vasudevan" # A string
4  print (value)
5  print (miles)
6  print (name)
```

Figure 1.16　Variables in Python.

Figure 1.17 Output for the code shown as Figure 1.16.

It is important to have a quick recap on the data types too:

- Any number like 1,2,4,100 can be called an integer.
- Bigger numbers like 468364387643864 should be called with respect. Means, it should be called Long Integers. Long integers should be represented by using l or L as a suffix!
- Any number such as 3.25 or 1.258 should be called a floating point number.
- Complex numbers are also supported. These look like 10 + 8i or −9 + 7i.

Let us navigate to the strings. Whatever is presented inside the single quote can be regarded as a string. An instance is 'Hello, World!', this is a string. One can understand from Figure 1.18 how strings work with Python.

Figure 1.18 Single quote and strings with Python.

Not only single quotes; double quotes are also fine for strings. "Hello, World!" is the same as 'Hello, World!' and one can refer to the screenshot presented below in Figure 1.19 with which readers can understand the scenario. Nevertheless, one thing to understand here is that one cannot mix up single quotes with double quotes and it would not work then.

```
C:\Users\Shriram K V>
C:\Users\Shriram K V>
C:\Users\Shriram K V>python
Python 3.6.5 (v3.6.5:f59c0932b4, Mar 28 2018, 17:00:18) [MSC v.1900 64 bit (AMD64)] on win32
Type "help", "copyright", "credits" or "license" for more information.
>>> 'Hello World'
'Hello World'
>>> print ('Hello world');
Hello World
>>> print ('Hello World')
Hello World
>>> "hello, world"          Same effect!!
'hello, world'
>>> print ("hello, world")
hello, world
>>> "hello, world'
  File "<stdin>", line 1     See, this!
    "hello, world'           You have to follow one pattern.. Can't keep mixing
                ^
SyntaxError: EOL while scanning string literal
>>>
```

Figure 1.19 Double quote and strings with Python.

Can we investigate triple quotes as an option? Do we even have triple quotes? One can include as many lines as possible (statements) with triple quotes being used. One can refer to Figure 1.20 to understand this concept.

```
Command Prompt - python
C:\Users\Shriram K V>python
Python 3.6.5 (v3.6.5:f59c0932b4, Mar 28 2018, 17:00:18) [MSC v.1900 64 bit (AMD64)] on win32
Type "help", "copyright", "credits" or "license" for more information.
>>> ''' Shriram is
... teaching you
... Python
... in an easier way '''
' Shriram is \nteaching you \nPython\nin an easier way '
>>> ''' Shriram is
... "Teaching you Python"
... in a 'easier' way!'''
' Shriram is \n"Teaching you Python" \nin a \'easier\' way!'
>>>
```

Figure 1.20 Triple quotes and strings with Python.

One can go ahead with concatenation of strings easily with Python. One can refer to Figure 1.21 to understand the string concatenation process. There is also an error, which is purposefully made, and the same is presented for the readers' perusal. One can see the purposeful error and the solution presented to understand the error.

```
File  Edit  Shell  Debug  Options  Window  Help
Python 3.11.5 (tags/v3.11.5:cce6ba9, Aug 24 2023, 14:38:34) [MSC v.1936 64 bit (AMD64)] on win32
Type "help", "copyright", "credits" or "license()" for more information.
>>> 'shriram is teaching' '.....' 'python to you all'
'shriram is teaching.....python to you all'
>>>
>>> 'shriram is teachin'.....'python to all'          Error
SyntaxError: invalid syntax
>>>
```

Figure 1.21 String concatenation with Python.

Can we learn unicode in Python? When you want to include the non-ASCII characters or your native language script as part of your program you must use "u". This means unicode. An example as always is handy and presented below in Figure 1.22 followed by the output presented in Figure 1.23.

```
1  x = u"i ♥♥♥♥♥♥ India"
2  print (x)
3
```

Figure 1.22   Unicode in Python.

```
Command Prompt

C:\Users\Shriram K V\Desktop\Python Playlist>python 2.py
i ♥♥♥♥♥♥ India
C:\Users\Shriram K V\Desktop\Python Playlist>
```

Figure 1.23   Output for the code presented in Figure 1.22.

However, one should also have a look at the code presented as Figure 1.24, which would certainly fail and the results are presented as in Figure 1.25.

```
1  ♥ = 10
2  print (♥)
3
```

Figure 1.24   Unicode usage – Failure scenario.

```
C:\Users\Shriram K V\Desktop\Python Playlist>python 2.py
  File "2.py", line 1
    ♥ = 10
    ^
SyntaxError: invalid character in identifier

C:\Users\Shriram K V\Desktop\Python Playlist>
```

Figure 1.25   Execution results for the code presented as Figure 1.24.

The escape sequences are the one to be discussed next and the sample code is presented in Figure 1.26, where all the escape sequences are included in the code. The results are presented in Figure 1.27 and one can refer to the same for enhanced understanding.

```
 1  print ("\n")
 2  tab_seq = "\t here you go with tab"
 3  new_line = "India is \n my country"
 4  back_space="Baa\bck space"
 5  back_slash="\\"
 6  form_feed="Hello_\fworld"
 7  single_quote="\'"
 8  double_quote="\""
 9  bell_ring="\a bell rings"
10  print (tab_seq)
11  print (new_line)
12  print (back_space)
13  print (form_feed)
14  print (single_quote)
15  print (double_quote)
16  print (bell_ring)
17  print (back_slash)
```

Figure 1.26   Escape sequences.

```
Command Prompt

C:\Users\Shriram K V\Desktop\Python Playlist>python 2.py

          here you go with tab
India is
 my country
Back space
Hello_□world
'
"
 bell rings
\

C:\Users\Shriram K V\Desktop\Python Playlist>
```

Figure 1.27   Execution result for the code presented in Figure 1.26.

Well, the first chapter is complete. Readers are expected to try these out practically. In addition, the readers can refer to the video links listed below for further understanding.

Python fundamentals – https://youtu.be/FgDWUV7_d2Q?si=v7UOltjhgSucfMPu

Execution of the code in Linux/String Operations – https://youtu.be/ZEWz2HFL1Lc?si=MlS3IziLMWzPZT51

Key Points to Remember

- Python has been growing tremendously and there is a lot of attention being paid to it.
- Python is simple and easy to use. It is very easy to understand a Python code and there is no complexity involved.
- Python is open source, and it is one of the very important reasons for its rapid growth and usage.
- Python can be used for building a variety of applications catering to different domains/sectors. One can build Machine Learning, Deep Learning, NLP, Data Analysis, Big Data, Automation, Embedded Applications and many more with Python. So, it is an ideal choice for anyone to learn.
- Python is excellently supported by massive and active developers. There are so many resources one could find for Python online.
- Python is available for all the known operating systems and platforms of which we are aware. It suits well for Windows, Linux and macOS.
- Python is most suitable for small-scale, medium-scale and large-scale applications.
- Python is a general-purpose programming language and is very easy to learn and use.
- Python is also regarded as an interpreted and high-level programming language which offers the users a lot of flexibility and versatility.
- Python uses the interpreter to execute the code. The interpreter reads the program and translates the same, line by line to machine code, then it can be executed. Make a note of the point, it happens line by line.

- Since the Python code is directly executed by the interpreter, there is no compilation step required as needed in C or C++.
- One can download Python for Windows or Mac. When it comes to Linux, Python is mostly pre-installed and if there is a requirement for an upgrade, it can easily be done.

Further Reading

Python official website – https://www.python.org/
Awesome Python – https://github.com/vinta/awesome-python

2

DEEPER LEARNING

LEARNING OBJECTIVES

After reading this chapter, the reader will have learned:

- More details on the variables and operations
- Boolean operations and Python
- How to do interactive programming with Python
- Keywords in Python
- Assertion, break and continue with Python
- Scope and related information
- Some interesting facts and points to remember.

2.1 Introduction

Having learnt the fundamentals in Chapter 1, it is time to enrich that learning through this chapter. More interesting stuff with examples shall be discussed in this chapter. It is always better to try out these things practically in parallel while learning.

2.2 Variables and More on Variables

Do we have anything special to know about the variables? Yes, we do. Following are the important points which someone should remember.

- It should start with a letter (character) or an underscore. (This means, you can't start a variable name otherwise).
- Value and value are not the same. _value and _Value is different.

DOI: 10.1201/9781032712673-2   **17**

One can refer to Figure 2.1 to understand the points quoted above. The code snippet and the results obtained during execution are presented as Figure 2.1. One could see the way the variable 'value' is presented in the code. _value, _Value, Value and value are different.

```
_value = 1;
_Value = 2;
Value = 1;
value = 2;
print (_value)
print (_Value)
print (Value)
print (value)
```

```
Command Prompt
C:\Users\Shriram K V\Desktop\Python Playlist>python 3.py
1
2
1
2

C:\Users\Shriram K V\Desktop\Python Playlist>
```

Figure 2.1 Variables and Python.

Interestingly, more than one _ (underscore) can be used in the variable name. Also, usage of _ _ continuously from the start is also accepted. One can see below the code snippet and results presented as Figure 2.2 to understand the aforesaid concept.

```
__value = 1
print (__value)
# here, we had two _

_value_one = 1;
print (_value_one)
```

```
Command Prompt
C:\Users\Shriram K V\Desktop\Python Playlist>python 4.py
1
1

C:\Users\Shriram K V\Desktop\Python Playlist>_
```

Figure 2.2 Variables with '_'.

One can observe that double underscores is usable and is not erroneous.

Remember, you are not permitted to use @, $ and % anywhere in the variable name. If this is done , it is an error and one can notice the same from Figure 2.3 where this is attempted.

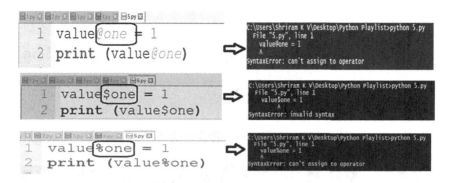

Figure 2.3 Variable naming guidelines.

It is now the time to try assigning and re-assigning values to the variables. One can understand the same by referring to Figure 2.4 where the code snippet and the results are presented.

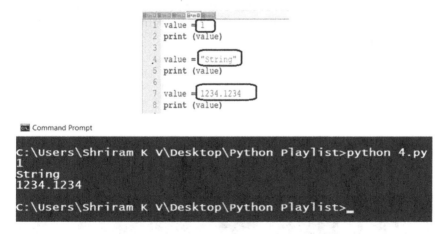

Figure 2.4 Variable value re-assignment.

Can we learn a little more? Yes, Python is just very comfortable. It lets you assign the same value to multiple variables in one shot.

Can we see if it does work? One can refer to Figure 2.5 to understand the aforesaid scenario.

```
1   value = 1;
2   value_1 = value_2 = value_3 = value
3   print (value)
4   print (value_1)
5   print (value_2)
6   print (value_3)
```

Command Prompt

```
C:\Users\Shriram K V\Desktop\Python Playlist>python 5.py
1
1
1
1

C:\Users\Shriram K V\Desktop\Python Playlist>
```

Figure 2.5   Same value assignment to multiple variables.

Multiple assignment in a single line is also possible with Python. One can have a look at Figure 2.6 where a sample code and results are presented.

```
1   value, value_1, value_2 = 1, 1.234, "Hello, World"
2   print (value)
3   print (value_1)
4   print (value_2)
```

Command Prompt

```
C:\Users\Shriram K V\Desktop\Python Playlist>python 5.py
1
1.234
Hello, World
C:\Users\Shriram K V\Desktop\Python Playlist>
```

Figure 2.6   Multiple assignment in a single line.

Is it possible to delete a variable? Yes, it is possible, and one can have a look at Figure 2.7 to understand the process of deletion and results are presented for improved understanding.

```
 1  value, value_1, value_2 = 1, 1.234, "Hello, World"
 2  print (value)
 3  print (value_1)
 4  print (value_2)
 5  del value
 6  del value_1
 7  del value_2
 8  print (value)
 9  print (value_1)
10  print (value_2)
```

```
Command Prompt

C:\Users\Shriram K V\Desktop\Python Playlist>python 5.py
1
1.234
Hello, World
Traceback (most recent call last):
  File "5.py", line 8, in <module>
    print (value)
NameError: name 'value' is not defined

C:\Users\Shriram K V\Desktop\Python Playlist>
```

Figure 2.7 Deletion of a variable.

Well, it is time for the readers to migrate to Boolean operations.

2.3 Boolean Operations with Python

Before we go deeper into Boolean operations with Python, it is important to answer a question. What is Boolean? Simply it must be one of the two – True or False. One needs no special guidelines to create Boolean variables. It is the same as the other variable types. One can see the code presented in Figure 2.8 to understand this better.

```
1  Boolean_Demo=True
2  print (Boolean_Demo)
3
4  Boolean_Demo=False
5  print (Boolean_Demo)
```

```
Command Prompt

C:\Users\Shriram K V\Desktop\Python Playlist>python 4.py
True
False

C:\Users\Shriram K V\Desktop\Python Playlist>
```

Figure 2.8 The Boolean operation.

One can understand the Boolean operations a bit better by referring to Figure 2.9. One can see the way things are tried and the results are presented for the readers' perusal.

Figure 2.9   The Boolean examples.

It is better to visualize everything as a code. One can refer to the code presented as Figure 2.10 and can understand the concept better.

```
print (1 == 1)
print (1 == 2)
print (1 <= 2)
print (1 >= 2)
print ("Sachin" == "Sachin")
print ("Sachin" != "Sachin")
print ("sachin" == "Sachin")
print (1.022 < 1.023)
print (1.022 > 1.023)
```

```
C:\Users\Shriram K V\Desktop\Python Playlist>python 4.py
True
False
True
False
True
False
False
True
False
```

Figure 2.10   The Boolean example as a code.

2.4 Interactive Programming with Python

One can also make the code interactive. This means the user can feed in the input on a real-time basis and the same can be processed. This will be interesting and, most importantly, is a great feature to be appreciated. One can see below the code presented as Figure 2.11 where the user is prompted for the input to be fed in and this makes it interactive. The execution result is presented as Figure 2.12.

```
1  print ("\n Hello, User! Welcome to the world of python")
2  print ("\n please enter your name")
3  name_user = input ("Enter your name")
4  print (name_user)
5  gender_user = input ("Can you please let me know your gender??")
6  print (gender_user)
7  print ("Hello, Mr." + name_user + " You are a " + gender_user )
```

Figure 2.11   The interactive programming with Python.

```
Command Prompt
C:\Users\Shriram K V\Desktop\Python Playlist>python 4.py

Hello, User! Welcome to the world of python

 please enter your name
Enter your name Shriram K V
 Shriram K V
Can you please let me know your gender?? Male
 Male
Hello, Mr. Shriram K V  You are a  Male

C:\Users\Shriram K V\Desktop\Python Playlist>_
```

Figure 2.12   Result for the execution of the code shown in Figure 2.11.

Remember this, input will always accept the feed as a string. Means, even you feed in the numbers as input, it goes ahead with it as a string.

2.5 Keywords in Python

Python uses reserved terms called keywords to determine the syntax and grammatical structure of the language. Because they are predefined in the language, these keywords cannot be used as identifiers (variable names, function names, etc.). One can have a look at the below list of keywords which are predefined. A brief note is also presented for quicker understanding:

- False: Represents the Boolean value False.
- None: Represents a null or undefined value.
- True: Represents the Boolean value True.
- and: Used for logical conjunction (&&).
- as: Used for aliasing while importing modules or creating context managers.
- assert: Used for debugging and testing purposes to assert that a condition is true.
- async: Indicates that a function or method is asynchronous.
- await: Used within asynchronous functions to wait for the completion of another asynchronous operation.
- break: Used to exit from a loop prematurely.
- class: Used to define a class.
- continue: Used to skip the current iteration of a loop and continue with the next one.
- def: Used to define a function or method.
- del: Used to delete variables, items from lists or attributes from objects.
- elif: Short for 'else if,' used in conditional statements.
- else: Used in conditional statements when the condition is not met.
- except: Used in exception handling to catch and handle exceptions.
- finally: Used in exception handling to specify a block of code that always executes, whether an exception is raised or not.
- for: Used to create a loop that iterates over a sequence (e.g., a list or a range).
- from: Used in import statements to specify which module to import.
- global: Used to declare a global variable within a function.
- if: Used for conditional statements.
- import: Used to import modules or specific items from modules.
- in: Used to check if a value is present in a sequence.

- is: Used for identity comparison (checking if two objects are the same).
- lambda: Used to create anonymous (nameless) functions.
- nonlocal: Used to declare a variable that is not local to the current function but also not global.
- not: Used for logical negation (!).
- or: Used for logical disjunction (||).
- pass: Used as a placeholder for code that does nothing.
- raise: Used to raise exceptions.
- return: Used to return a value from a function.
- try: Used in exception handling to start a block of code where exceptions are monitored.
- while: Used to create a loop that continues if a condition is true.
- with: Used to create a context manager.
- yield: Used in generator functions to yield a value to the caller.

Most of these keywords shall be used in the entire book in a place or other and the readers can easily understand the usage. However, the readers shall be exposed to some of the keywords in the subsequent discussions.

2.5.1 *Let's Test 'and', 'or' and 'not'*

One can see from Figure 2.13 that True and False has given the result as False. Similarly, True and True has yielded the result True. One can try this out.

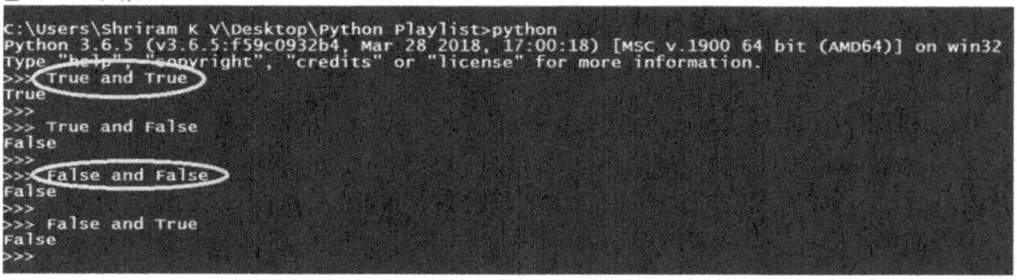

Figure 2.13 'and' in Python.

Similarly, one can try out 'or'. One can refer to Figure 2.14 to understand how 'or' works. True or True is True, False or False is False. Readers can try this out as well.

```
>>>
>>> True or True
True
>>> False or True
True
>>> True or False
True
>>> False or False
False
>>> _
```

Figure 2.14   'or' in Python.

The next one in the queue is not. Yes, it is simple to understand. This is because not is an inversion: The not of true is false and vice versa. One can have a look below at Figure 2.15 to understand not better.

```
Command Prompt - python
C:\Users\shriram K V\Desktop\Python Playlist>python
Python 3.6.5 (v3.6.5:f59c0932b4, Mar 28 2018, 17:00:18) [MSC v.1900 64 bit (AMD64)] on win32
Type "help", "copyright", "credits" or "license" for more information.
>>> not (True)
False
>>> not (False)
True
>>> not (1)
False
>>> not (0)
True
>>> _
```

Figure 2.15   'not' in Python.

2.5.2 'break' and Continue

Like other programming languages, Python also supports both break and continue. Break and continue are used inside 'for' and 'while' loops to alter their normal behaviour. In Python, the break statement is a control flow statement that is used to exit a loop prematurely. It is typically used within loops, such as for loops and while loops, to terminate the loop execution based on a certain condition.

An example shall always be handy, and we present this in Figure 2.16. One can understand the way break works by referring to the example presented. For and while loops will be discussed at a later point in time.

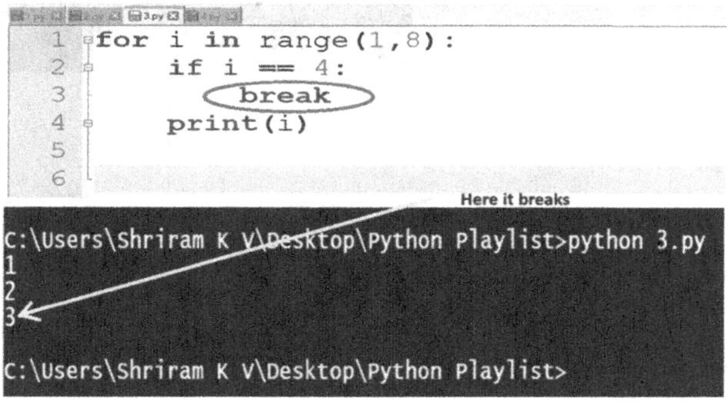

Figure 2.16 'break' in Python.

One more example shall assist readers in understanding the usage of the break better. One can refer to Figure 2.17 to have a look at another instance of how break has been used.

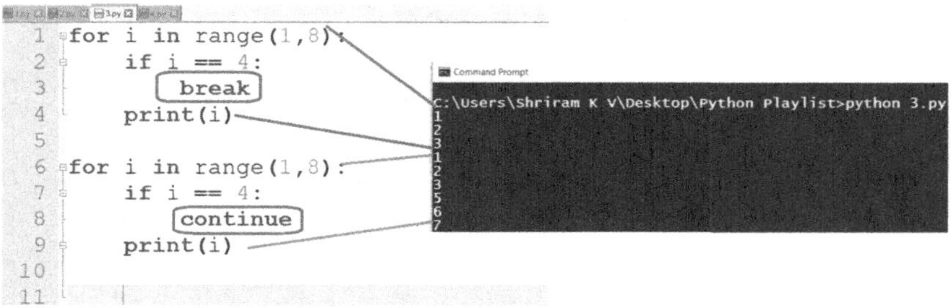

Figure 2.17 'break' in Python – another instance.

Can we work with the if and elif now? if and elif (short for 'else if') are conditional statements used for making decisions in your code. They allow you to execute different blocks of code based on certain conditions. One can have a look at Figure 2.18 where the usage of if and elif is clearly presented.

```
 1  print ('iteration one')
 2  print ('*************')
 3  a = 1
 4  if a == 1:
 5      print('One')
 6  elif a == 2:
 7      print('Two')
 8  else:
 9      print('Something else')
10
11  print ('iteration two')
12  print ('*************')
13  a = 5
14  if a == 1:
15      print('One')
16  elif a == 2:
17      print('Two')
18  else:
19      print('Something else')
20
```

```
Command Prompt
C:\Users\Shriram K V\Desktop\Python Playlist>python 3.py
iteration one
*************
One
iteration two
*************
Something else

C:\Users\Shriram K V\Desktop\Python Playlist>
```

Figure 2.18 'if' and 'elif'.

2.5.3 Global Scope in Python

The next important thing to learn is scoping in Python. As always, an example shall be handy and the same is presented as Figure 2.19, where the readers can understand the scoping concept.

```
global_variable=10
def fun1():
    print (global_variable)
def fun2():
    global_variable = 5
    print (global_variable)


fun1();
fun2();
fun1();
```

Figure 2.19 Global scope.

Remember if you assign value to a variable inside a function, it is called local scope. If you assign value to a variable outside all the functions, it is called the global scope.

One can see that global_variable is appropriately called in two different functions fun1() and fun2(). One can see the results presented in Figure 2.20, where the way the global scope works can be clearly understood. The programmer is free to redefine the global_variable inside the function as required.

```
Python 3.11.5 (tags/v3.11.5:cce6ba9, Aug 24 2023, 14:38:34) [MSC v.1936 64 bit
AMD64)] on win32
Type "help", "copyright", "credits" or "license()" for more information.

= RESTART: C:/Users/shriramk/AppData/Local/Programs/Python/Python311/test.py
10
5
10
|
```

Figure 2.20   Execution result for the code presented as Figure 2.19.

2.5.4 'is' in Python

'is' is used in Python for testing object identity. One can have a look at Figure 2.21 below to understand the way 'is' is used.

```
Command Prompt - python
C:\Users\Shriram K V\Desktop\Python Playlist>python
Python 3.6.5 (v3.6.5:f59c0932b4, Mar 28 2018, 17:00:18) [MSC v.1900 64 bit (AMD64)] on win32
Type "help", "copyright", "credits" or "license" for more information.
>>> True is True
True
>>> True is False
False
>>> False is True
False
>>> False is False
True
>>>
```

Figure 2.21   'is' in Python.

Well, the readers have been presented with more fundamentals in this chapter. More learning awaits in the subsequent chapter, and it will be a fun ride.

Key Points to Remember

- One can assign the same value to multiple variables in one shot.
- Multiple assignment in a single line is also possible with Python.
- Is it possible to delete a variable? Yes, it is possible.

- Python uses reserved terms called keywords to determine the syntax and grammatical structure of the language.
- Break and continue are used inside 'for' and 'while' loops to alter their normal behaviour.
- if and elif (short for 'else if') are conditional statements used for making decisions in your code.
- if you assign value to a variable inside a function, it is called local scope. If you assign value to a variable outside all the functions, it is called global scope.
- 'is' is used in Python for testing object identity.

Further Reading

For further learning one can refer to:

Python official website – https://www.python.org/
Awesome Python – https://github.com/vinta/awesome-python

One can also walk through below the videos to understand things better.

Naming conventions, variables with Python, multiple assignment – https://youtu.be/kvPYmN2HG8A
Keywords in Python with demo – https://youtu.be/RRVeKstM0jk
Keywords in Python with demo – https://youtu.be/QW2efyeN670

3

LEARNING GETS BETTER

LEARNING OBJECTIVES

After reading this chapter, the reader will have learned about:

- Tuples in Python
- Lists in Python
- The decision control statement
- Pass in Python and
- Some interesting facts and points to remember.

3.1 Introduction

Readers have been introduced to a lot of fundamental concepts with example codes. We request the readers try the codes practically to get an enhanced understanding. In this chapter, readers shall be presented with the tuples, lists, decision control statements and, finally, pass. All of these are interesting and easy to understand. We shall begin with tuples.

3.2 Tuples in Python

It is simple and powerful which works just like list in the Python (Don't worry, we shall handle the lists in the subsequent section). The only thing the readers need to remember is tuple is a read-only datatype, which means that it is one time write. Also, there are some confusions regarding tuples vs. arrays. Tuples are not arrays. Array has only one data type content permitted to be inside and here it is flexible in the tuples. One can understand the usage of tuples through the example presented as Figure 3.1, with results also being included.

One could see from Figure 3.1 the clear usage of tuples. Remember, Tuple is case-sensitive.

DOI: 10.1201/9781032712673-3

```
1  #Tup represents tuples in python! This is case sensitive, friends.
2  Tup = (1, 2, 3, 4)
3  print (Tup)
4  print (Tup [0])
5  print (Tup [1])
6  print (Tup [0:3])
```

```
Microsoft Windows [Version 10.0.17134.706]
(c) 2018 Microsoft Corporation. All rights reserved.

C:\Users\Shriram K V>cd Desktop

C:\Users\Shriram K V\Desktop>cd "Python Playlist"

C:\Users\Shriram K V\Desktop\Python Playlist>python 7.py
(1, 2, 3, 4)
1
2
(1, 2, 3)
```

Figure 3.1   Tuples in Python.

One more example which is slightly complex is presented as Figure 3.2 with results. One can see the versatility that tuples bring to the

```
1  #Tup represents tuples in python! This is case sensitive, friends.
2  Tup = (1, 2, 3, 4)
3  print (Tup)
4  print (Tup [0])
5  print (Tup [1])
6  print (Tup [0:3])
7  print ('***********')
8  Tup2 = ('a', 'b', 'c')
9  print (Tup2)
10 print (Tup2 [0])
11 print (Tup2 [1])
12 print (Tup2 [0:2])
```

Command Prompt

```
C:\Users\Shriram K V\Desktop\Python Playlist>python 7.py
(1, 2, 3, 4)
1
2
(1, 2, 3)
***********
('a', 'b', 'c')
a
b
('a', 'b')
```

Figure 3.2   Tuple example in Python.

table through the example below. Readers should clearly understand the way Tup has been used. We reiterate that, Tup is case-sensitive.

One can even double the tuples. Yes, it is possible. Readers can refer to the code presented in Figure 3.3 to understand the same. The results reveal the double tuple.

```
1  #Tup represents tuples in python! This is case sensitive, friends.
2  Tup = (1, 2, 3, 4)
3  print (Tup)
4  print (Tup [0])
5  print (Tup [1])
6  print (Tup [0:3])
7  print ('Lets double the tuples')
8  print (Tup * 2)
```

Command Prompt

```
C:\Users\Shriram K V\Desktop\Python Playlist>python 7.py
(1, 2, 3, 4)
1
2
(1, 2, 3)
Lets double the tuples
(1, 2, 3, 4, 1, 2, 3, 4)
```

Figure 3.3   Double the tuple.

One can also concatenate two tuples together. This is easier for readers to understand through an example, as shown in Figure 3.4 with results. Tuples provide a lot of flexibility and comfort to programmers.

```
1  #Tup represents tuples in python! This is case sensitive, friends.
2  Tup = (1, 2, 3, 4)
3  print (Tup)
4  print (Tup [0])
5  print (Tup [1])
6  print (Tup [0:3])
7  print ('Lets Concatenate')
8  Tup2 = (1.0, 2.0, 3.0, 4.0)
9  print (Tup + Tup2)
```

Command Prompt

```
C:\Users\Shriram K V\Desktop\Python Playlist>python 7.py
(1, 2, 3, 4)
1
2
(1, 2, 3)
Lets Concatenate
(1, 2, 3, 4, 1.0, 2.0, 3.0, 4.0)

C:\Users\Shriram K V\Desktop\Python Playlist>
```

Figure 3.4   Tuple concatenation.

Well, it is time to navigate to the lists next.

3.3 Lists in Python

It is very important to know the differences between lists and tuples in Python. Though they appear similar, there are some key differences to be understood.

First, mutability. Lists are mutable. Understanding the term mutability is important here. Mutability means that one can change their content after the lists are created. By contrast, tuples are immutable; once a tuple is created, one cannot change its elements. One cannot add, remove or modify elements in the tuple. Similarly, lists are defined with square brackets whereas tuples are defined with parenthesis. An example may prove helpful here. Readers can refer to Figure 3.5 to understand the same.

```
1  list = [1, 2, 3, 4]
2  print (list)
3  print (list [0])
4  print (list [1])
5  list = ['S','H','R','I','R','A','M']
6  print (list)
```

```
Command Prompt

C:\Users\Shriram K V\Desktop\Python Playlist>python 8.py
[1, 2, 3, 4]
1
2
['S', 'H', 'R', 'I', 'R', 'A', 'M']
C:\Users\Shriram K V\Desktop\Python Playlist>
```

Figure 3.5   Lists in Python.

One can clearly see the differences between lists and tuples clearly from the above example. The next topic to be learnt is the decision control statements in Python. This is certainly very interesting and also easy for readers to understand.

3.4 Decision Control Statements

Well, as we know, decision control statements are used to transfer the control of execution from one location to another based on meeting the requirements. Two well-known statements are to be seen first. These are:

- If statement.
- If – else statement.

Let's start with the 'if' statement and then navigate to 'if – else'.

The syntax for the 'if' statement, and the flow, is presented in Figure 3.6.

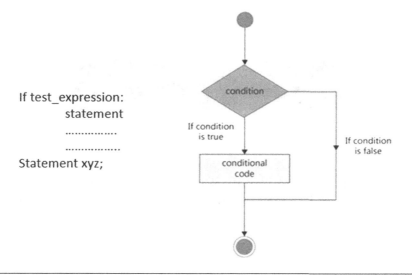

Figure 3.6 'if' statement in Python.

A simple code to increment a number by 6 if the number is greater than 2 is presented below as Figure 3.7 along with results.

```
1  #code for if condition
2  p = 2
3  if (p >= 2):
4      p = p+6
5      print (p)
6  #statements after the if, this will be reached after executing the if.
7  print ("this is an if demo")
```

```
Command Prompt
C:\Users\Shriram K V\Desktop\Python Playlist>python if_test.py
8
this is an if demo

C:\Users\Shriram K V\Desktop\Python Playlist>
```

Figure 3.7 An instance for the 'if' statement.

One more instance where the condition is not met is also presented as Figure 3.8.

One more example is presented below.

```
1  #code for if condition
2  p = 2
3  if (p >= 3):
4      p = p+6
5      print (p)
6  #statements after the if, this will be reached after executing the if.
7  print ("this is an if demo")
```

```
Command Prompt

C:\Users\Shriram K V\Desktop\Python Playlist>python if_test.py
this is an if demo

C:\Users\Shriram K V\Desktop\Python Playlist>cls_
```

Figure 3.8   'if' statement example.

Write a program to identify if the user has entered character or integer as input. Use the input function as you require. (Please note, we have used isdigit and isalpha in this example as presented in Figure 3.9.)

```
1  char = input ("hello user, enter a character/integer \t")
2  if (char.isdigit()):
3      print ("Hello boss, you have entered a number")
4  if (char.isalpha()):
5      print ("Hello boss, you have entered a character")
```

```
Command Prompt

C:\Users\Shriram K V\Desktop\Python Playlist>python if_demo.py
hello user, enter a character/integer   3
Hello boss, you have entered a number

C:\Users\Shriram K V\Desktop\Python Playlist>python if_demo.py
hello user, enter a character/integer   d
Hello boss, you have entered a character

C:\Users\Shriram K V\Desktop\Python Playlist>python if_demo.py
hello user, enter a character/integer      *

C:\Users\Shriram K V\Desktop\Python Playlist>
```

Figure 3.9   'if' statement example – 2.

It is time to learn the if – else's usage now.

The syntax is presented below to the readers for enhanced understanding.

If (test_expression):
   statement 1
else
   statement 2
Statement xyz;

One can understand the way in which if – else works by having a look at the syntax above. If the test expression is true, statement 1 shall be evaluated; otherwise, it will move to the else block. One can consider Figure 3.10 to understand the functioning of if – else.

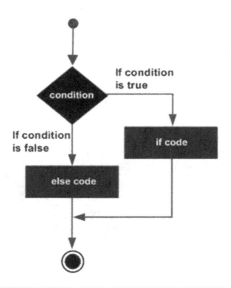

Figure 3.10   The 'if – else' workflow.

One example shall be very helpful here. A program to let the user enter a number as input, If the number is <10, tell him hello. Else, tell him, hi is written using the if – else structure. The code and the results are presented as Figure 3.11.

```
1  number = int(input("hello user, enter a number \t"))
2  if (number < 10):
3      print ("The number is below 10")
4  else:
5      print ("You entered a number above 10")
6  print ("this will run irrespective of any condition")
```

```
Command Prompt

C:\Users\Shriram K V\Desktop\Python Playlist>python if_else.py
hello user, enter a number          5
The number is below 10
this will run irrespective of any condition

C:\Users\Shriram K V\Desktop\Python Playlist>python if_else.py
hello user, enter a number          11
You entered a number above 10
this will run irrespective of any condition
```

Figure 3.11   The 'if – else' example–1.

One more example to check if the entered number is odd or even is presented below as Figure 3.12.

```
1  number = int(input("hello user, enter a number \t"))
2  if (number%2==0):
3      print ("The number is Even")
4  else:
5      print ("The number is Odd")
6  print ("this will run irrespective of any condition")
7
```

```
Command Prompt

C:\Users\Shriram K V\Desktop\Python Playlist>python if_else.py
hello user, enter a number          6
The number is Even
this will run irrespective of any condition

C:\Users\Shriram K V\Desktop\Python Playlist>python if_else.py
hello user, enter a number          5
The number is Odd
this will run irrespective of any condition
```

Figure 3.12   The 'if – else' example–2.

From the two examples above, one could understand the usage of if – else. We recommend the readers to try these out practically to gain more in-depth knowledge.

Readers would have gotten a query by now. Can the if's be nested and used? Will that be feasible? The answer is yes. One can refer to Figure 3.13 to understand the usage of nested if's. The results are also presented for easier understanding.

```
 1  mark = int(input("Hello Student,Please enter your marks \t"))
 2  if mark >= 50 and mark <= 100:
 3      print ("Congrats, you have passed with P grade")
 4  else:
 5      if mark <=49:
 6          print ("Am sorry, you failed")
 7      else:
 8          print ("Please enter correct input")
 9  # Be Careful with the indentation!!
```

```
Command Prompt

C:\Users\Shriram K V\Desktop\Python Playlist>python 10.py
Hello Student,Please enter your marks      105
Please enter correct input

C:\Users\Shriram K V\Desktop\Python Playlist>python 10.py
Hello Student,Please enter your marks      100
Congrats, you have passed with P grade

C:\Users\Shriram K V\Desktop\Python Playlist>
```

Figure 3.13   Nested 'if'.

It is also important to understand the usage of elif. elif enables multi way selection without hassle. An example would help in the understanding and the same is presented as Figure 3.14 with code and result.

```
 1  mark = int(input("Hello Student,Please enter your marks (0-100) \t"))
 2  if mark >=80 and mark <=100:
 3      print ("Congrats, Distinction")
 4  elif mark >=70:
 5      print ("Congrats, A grade")
 6  elif mark >=60:
 7      print ("Congrats, B grade")
 8  elif mark >=50:
 9      print ("Congrats, C grade")
10  else:
11      print ("Fail")
```

```
Select Command Prompt

C:\Users\Shriram K V\Desktop\Python Playlist>python 11.py
Hello Student,Please enter your marks (0-100)     65
Congrats, B grade

C:\Users\Shriram K V\Desktop\Python Playlist>python 11.py
Hello Student,Please enter your marks (0-100)     76
Congrats, A grade

C:\Users\Shriram K V\Desktop\Python Playlist>python 11.py
Hello Student,Please enter your marks (0-100)     100
Congrats, Distinction

C:\Users\Shriram K V\Desktop\Python Playlist>python 11.py
Hello Student,Please enter your marks (0-100)     43
Fail
```

Figure 3.14   'elif' – an example.

It is time for a simple exercise to be tried out. Let us calculate the number of days in a month. User must input the month number as input(1 for January, 2 for February, etc.). One can use if, else, elif as preferred.

Disclaimer: One can try out different logics to accomplish this task. Here the readers are presented with one such logic for building the solution for the given problem statement (Figure 3.15).

```
1  month = int(input("Hello User, Enter the month you want to find the number of
   days in (1-12) \t"))
2  if  month == 2:
3      print ("Welcome to Feb, 28 days for normal year, 29 for leap")
4  elif month in (1, 3, 5, 7, 8, 10, 12):
5      print ("You have 31 days!")
6  elif month in (4, 6, 9, 11):
7      print ("You have 30 days")
8  else:
9      print ("You have entered wrong values, Check")
10
```

```
C:\Users\Shriram K V\Desktop\Python Playlist>python 12.py
Hello User, Enter the month you want to find the number of days in (1-12)    45
You have entered wrong values, Check

C:\Users\Shriram K V\Desktop\Python Playlist>python 12.py
Hello User, Enter the month you want to find the number of days in (1-12)    12
You have 31 days!

C:\Users\Shriram K V\Desktop\Python Playlist>python 12.py
Hello User, Enter the month you want to find the number of days in (1-12)    1
You have 31 days!

C:\Users\Shriram K V\Desktop\Python Playlist>python 12.py
Hello User, Enter the month you want to find the number of days in (1-12)    2
Welcome to Feb, 28 days for normal year, 29 for leap

C:\Users\Shriram K V\Desktop\Python Playlist>python 12.py
Hello User, Enter the month you want to find the number of days in (1-12)    4
You have 30 days
```

Figure 3.15 Example with Python decision control statements.

Enough of the ifs and elifs. Let us learn while for a while now. The syntax for while and the workflow for the same is presented as Figure 3.16.

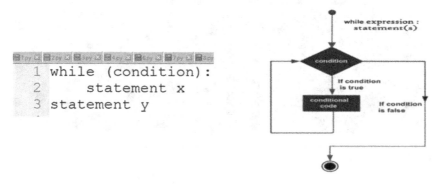

```
1  while (condition):
2      statement x
3  statement y
```

Figure 3.16 'while' – syntax and workflow.

One can understand the way while works by referring to Figure 3.16. If the condition is true, then the statement x will work; else, it would be statement y.

An example would be very helpful here. Let's print the first 15 whole numbers! But, with while. The code is presented as Figure 3.17, which also has results presented.

```
1  i = 0
2  while (i <=15):
3      print (i)
4      i =i + 1
```

Figure 3.17 Example – 'while'.

One should understand this point – Indentation has a huge respect to be given and readers should never forget this point.

It is important to go ahead with the for loop now. Readers must be familiar with the usage of for with other programming languages, but it's time to learn it with Python as well.

The syntax and the workflow are presented as Figure 3.18.

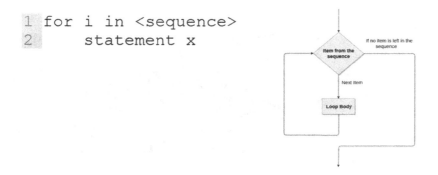

```
1  for i in <sequence>
2      statement x
```

Figure 3.18 'for' – syntax and workflow.

An instance shall be helpful here. Below the code snippet presented (Figure 3.19) has a simple for loop used and the results are presented for the readers' perusal.

```
for i in [1, 2, 3, 4]:
    print (i)
    i = i + 2
    print (i)
print ("I am done")
```

Command Prompt

```
C:\Users\Shriram K V\Desktop\Python Playlist>python 14.py
1
3
2
4
3
5
4
6
I am done
```

Figure 3.19 An instance with 'for'.

It is very important to know the usage of the range() function. An instance is presented below as Figure 3.20.

```
for i in range(1, 5):
    print (i)
print ("I am done")
```

Command Prompt

```
C:\Users\Shriram K V\Desktop\Python Playlist>python 15.py
1
2
3
4
I am done

C:\Users\Shriram K V\Desktop\Python Playlist>_
```

Figure 3.20 'range' usage.

One more example with range is presented as Figure 3.21.

```
1  i = 0
2  sum = 0
3  for i in range(1, 11):
4      sum = sum + i
5      i =i + 1
6  print (sum)
```

Command Prompt

```
C:\Users\Shriram K V\Desktop\Python Playlist>python 16.py
55

C:\Users\Shriram K V\Desktop\Python Playlist>
```

Figure 3.21   'range' usage – another instance.

Once again, readers are prompted to try these out practically to get more understanding. It is time to learn about pass in Python.

Pass is like NOP (or no operation) in microprocessors. This is helpful, when a statement is needed in a code for syntactical presence and not for any other meaningful execution.

A simple example is presented below as Figure 3.22.

1.py - C:/Users/Saihari Shriram/Desktop/Python Files/1.py (3.7.3)

File   Edit   Format   Run   Options   Window   Help

```
print ("hello")
pass #this is no operation folks!
print ("done")
```

Python 3.7.3 Shell

File   Edit   Shell   Debug   Options   Window   Help

```
Python 3.7.3 (v3.7.3:ef4ec6ed12, Mar 25 2019, 22:22:05) [MSC v.1916 64 bit (AMD64)] on
Type "help", "copyright", "credits" or "license()" for more information.
>>>
======== RESTART: C:/Users/Saihari Shriram/Desktop/Python Files/1.py ========
hello
done
>>>
```

Figure 3.22   'pass' in Python.

There is an interesting feature available in Python. else cannot be used with while/for in other programming languages such as C or C++. In Python, however, this is possible. An instance is presented as Figure 3.23, where else is used with while.

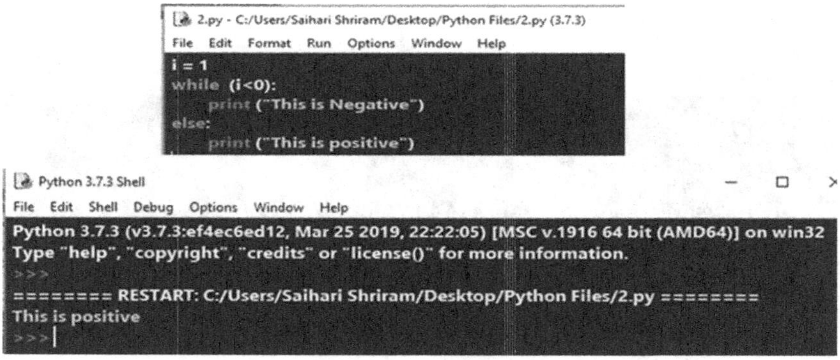

```
i = 1
while (i<0):
    print ("This is Negative")
else:
    print ("This is positive")
```

```
Python 3.7.3 (v3.7.3:ef4ec6ed12, Mar 25 2019, 22:22:05) [MSC v.1916 64 bit (AMD64)] on win32
Type "help", "copyright", "credits" or "license()" for more information.
>>>
======== RESTART: C:/Users/Saihari Shriram/Desktop/Python Files/2.py ========
This is positive
>>>
```

Figure 3.23   'else' with 'while'.

Similarly, else is used with for in the example presented as Figure 3.24.

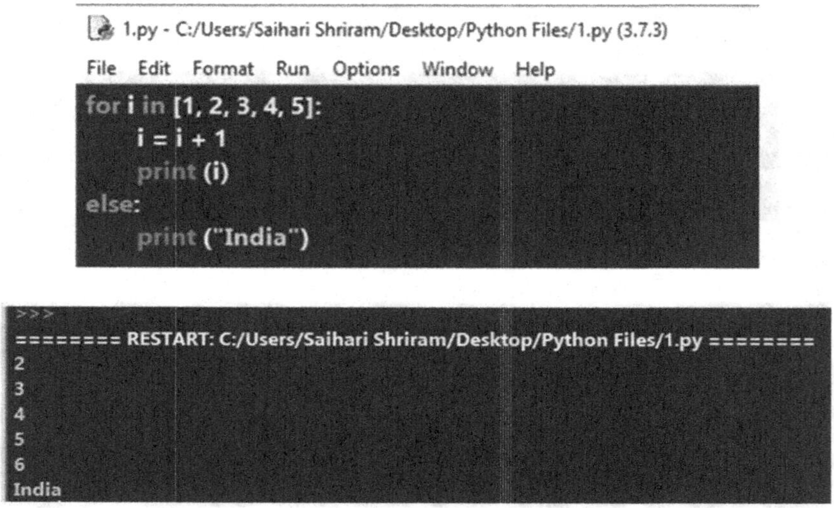

```
for i in [1, 2, 3, 4, 5]:
    i = i + 1
    print (i)
else:
    print ("India")
```

```
>>>
======== RESTART: C:/Users/Saihari Shriram/Desktop/Python Files/1.py ========
2
3
4
5
6
India
```

Figure 3.24   'else' with 'for'.

Readers shall be introduced to functions in the subsequent chapter. The journey is going to get more interesting and exciting.

Readers can watch the following YouTube lectures to gain more understanding:

Tuples and lists – https://youtu.be/0FJ2cfJrWLc?si=IvBcLkZ9 7YsYdfVd

If, elif, else – if, while, range – https://youtu.be/ucYzxhALs1Y?si= 9qV4-4SV_0z_zifD

Pass in Python – https://youtu.be/9ArlSaO_q6c?si=tTSz-vc PP2w66O76

Key Points to Remember

- Tuple is a read-only datatype, which means that it is one time write.
- Tuples are not arrays. Array has only one data type content permitted to be inside and here it is flexible in the tuples.
- Lists are mutable.
- Tuples are immutable, meaning that once a tuple is created one cannot change its elements. One cannot add, remove or modify elements in the tuple.
- Two well-known statements supported in Python are the if statement and the if – else statement.
- While and for are also supported and the beauty is, with for or while one can use else in Python.
- Pass is like NOP (no operation) in microprocessors. This is helpful, when a statement is needed in a code for syntactical presence and not for any other meaningful execution.

Further Reading

Python official website – https://www.python.org/
Awesome Python – https://github.com/vinta/awesome-python

4

FUNCTIONS – IN AND OUT

LEARNING OBJECTIVES

After reading this chapter, reader will have learned:
- The need for functions
- Usage of the functions
- Nested and lambda functions and
- Some interesting facts and points to remember.

4.1 Introduction

Functions are one of the most important aspects of any programming language. Functions are very important for the following reasons. Functions provide:

- Modularity – One can break a complex issue into a smaller one easily when the functions-based approach is followed. This makes the life of a programmer a lot easier.
- Abstraction – Another very important aspect of the functions is that it abstracts the implementation details of a particular operation. When someone calls or uses the function, there is no need to know how the function has been built.
- Readability – Well-written functions are always appreciable. It enhances the code's readability and makes the code more self-explanatory.
- Reusability – The functions also promote code reusability. One need not reinvent the wheel. Once a function is written

DOI: 10.1201/9781032712673-4

and tested, it can be reused any number of times as required. This will save both time and effort.

- Debugging – Functions help in isolating and debugging issues in your code, enabling the programmer to focus on the issue much more clearly.
- Testing – Functions make it easier to write unit tests, as you can test each function in isolation. This makes testing both more effective and more efficient.
- Maintainability – When a situation arises where one needs to make changes or improvements to the code, it can be done with ease focusing on one function at a time without affecting any other functions.
- Collaboration – Numerous developers frequently focus on various areas of the codebase in larger software development projects. By establishing distinct boundaries and interfaces for various software components, functions promote greater collaboration. This is the biggest advantage one could cite while using functions.
- Code organization – Functions facilitate logical code organization. Your program's structure can be easier to manage and comprehend by breaking off similar functionality into distinct functions.

Looking at all the above points, readers would have understood the importance of functions. Python supports functions and readers will be provided with all of the details in the subsequent sections.

4.2 Functions in Python

Whenever needed, the function can be invoked (any number of times). On exit from a function, it will go to the place where it must (Next line of code). Python has many built-in functions, but programmers can also define their own functions. People also call functions subroutines. There is no limit with respect to the number of functions one can define in a program. The function block should start with the def keyword. The keyword is followed by a function name of the programmer's choice and a parenthesis should follow. The code inside the function defined by programmer is his/her responsibility. One should make sure that the indentation is all properly done inside the code block too.

The syntax is presented below:

def fun_name (parameters ....):
        function_content
        .....
        .....
    next_line

Any function should return a value and we shall try this as well in the example as shown in Figure 4.1. One can see the way the functions add and sub have been defined. Also, one should observe the way the functions are called.

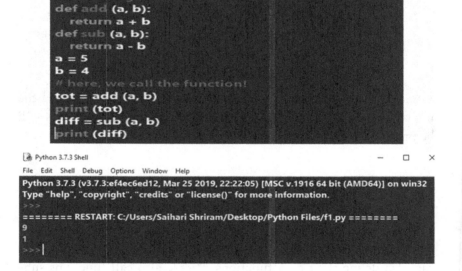

Figure 4.1 Functions – Definition and call.

For the readers, a very simple programming exercise with which one can print a name ten times is presented below as Figure 4.2.

```
File  Edit  Format  Run  Options  Window  Help
def fun_print ():
    i = 0
    while (i < 10):
        print ("Sachin Tendulkar")
        i=i+1
fun_print()
```

```
Python 3.7.3 (v3.7.3:ef4ec6ed12, Mar 25 2019, 22:22:05) [MSC v.1916 64 bit (AMD64)] on win32
Type "help", "copyright", "credits" or "license()" for more information.
>>>
======== RESTART: C:/Users/Saihari Shriram/Desktop/Python Files/f2.py ========
Sachin Tendulkar
Sachin Tendulkar
Sachin Tendulkar
Sachin Tendulkar
Sachin Tendulkar
Sachin Tendulkar
Sachin Tendulkar
Sachin Tendulkar
Sachin Tendulkar
Sachin Tendulkar
>>>
```

Figure 4.2 Function to print a name.

Next, the readers are presented with a sample code where the "call by values" approach is followed. One can refer to Figure 4.3, where the code and results are presented.

```
File  Edit  Format  Run  Options  Window  Help
# here we go with the function definition first.
def add (a, b):
    return a + b
def sub (a, b):
    return a - b
x = 5
y = 4
# here, we call the function!
tot = add (x,y)
print (tot)
diff = sub (x, y)
print (diff)
```

```
Python 3.7.3 (v3.7.3:ef4ec6ed12, Mar 25 2019, 22:22:05) [MSC v.1916 64 bit (AMD64)] on win32
Type "help", "copyright", "credits" or "license()" for more information.
>>>
======== RESTART: C:\Users\Saihari Shriram\Desktop\Python Files\f1.py ========
9
1
>>>
```

Figure 4.3 Functions with call by value approach.

Can expressions be passed to a function? Yes, it can be. One can have a look at Figure 4.4, where an expression has been passed to a function.

```
File  Edit  Format  Run  Options  Window  Help
def fun_demo (x):
    print ("Here you go", x)
fun_demo (3+3*2)
```

```
Python 3.7.3 Shell                                              □  :
File  Edit  Shell  Debug  Options  Window  Help
Python 3.7.3 (v3.7.3:ef4ec6ed12, Mar 25 2019, 22:22:05) [MSC v.1916 64 bit (AMD64)] on win32
Type "help", "copyright", "credits" or "license()" for more information.
>>>
======== RESTART: C:/Users/Saihari Shriram/Desktop/Python Files/f3.py ========
Here you go 9
>>>
```

Figure 4.4 Expressions passed to a function.

It is time to make the functions interactive. Let's take 2 integers as input from user. Let's multiply, add and divide the input values with each other. One can also see the actual vs. formal parameters been highlighted in Figure 4.5.

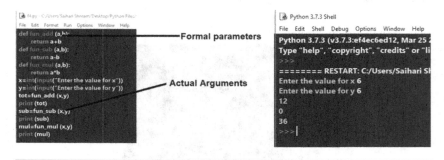

Figure 4.5 Interactive functions.

Can a function return more than one return value? Technically, in other programming languages it may not be possible. Can we try this out in Python? Results would be really interesting and the same is presented in Figure 4.6. One could observe that the function has returned 2 values.

```
File  Edit  Format  Run  Options  Window  Help
def fun_demo (temp_week_data):
    return (max (temp_week_data), min (temp_week_data))
# the above is the function definition.
#lets get into the function call
temp_data=[30, 32, 34, 34, 45, 53]
max= fun_demo(temp_data)
print (max)
```

```
File  Edit  Shell  Debug  Options  Window  Help
Python 3.7.3 (v3.7.3:ef4ec6ed12, Mar 25 2019, 22:22:05) [MSC v.1916 64 bit (AMD64)] on
Type "help", "copyright", "credits" or "license()" for more information.
>>>
======== RESTART: C:/Users/Saihari Shriram/Desktop/Python Files/f5.py ========
(53, 30)
>>>
```

Figure 4.6 Function returning more than one value.

One should know the default assignments for the functions with Python. This provides a default value if a value is not assigned during the function call (one can connect this with the default constructor concept from the C++) (Figure 4.7).

```
File  Edit  Format  Run  Options  Window  Help
def fun_demo (age, country="India"):
    print (age)
    print (country)
                                        Default Value.
fun_demo(age='15')
fun_demo(age='20', country='USA')
```

```
File  Edit  Shell  Debug  Options  Window  Help
Python 3.11.5 (tags/v3.11.5:cce6ba9, Aug 24 2023, 14:38:34) [MSC v.1936 64 bi
t (AMD64)] on win32
Type "help", "copyright", "credits" or "license()" for more information.
>>>
= RESTART: C:/Users/shriramk/AppData/Local/Programs/Python/Python311/2.py
15
India
20
USA
```

Figure 4.7 Default value demonstration.

Can we have variable length arguments in Python? Yes, it is possible, and an instance is presented as Figure 4.8 with the use of variable length arguments. One can see that the number of arguments are 3, 2 and 5, respectively.

```
File  Edit  Format  Run  Options  Window  Help
def fun_demo (name, *Sportsperson):
    print ("\n", name, "likes the players")
    for subject in Sportsperson:
        print (subject)
fun_demo("Sachin", "Dravid", "MSD")
fun_demo ("Sachin", "Lara")
fun_demo ("Gayle", "MSD", "Sachin", "Kumble", "Pandya")
```

```
File  Edit  Shell  Debug  Options  Window  Help
Python 3.7.3 (v3.7.3:ef4ec6ed12, Mar 25 2019, 22:22:05) [MSC v.1916 64 bit (AMD64)] on win32
Type "help", "copyright", "credits" or "license()" for more information.
>>>
======== RESTART: C:/Users/Saihari Shriram/Desktop/Python Files/f8.py ========

Sachin likes the players
Dravid
MSD

Sachin likes the players
Lara

Gayle likes the players
MSD
Sachin
Kumble
Pandya
```

Figure 4.8   Variable length arguments.

It's time to learn nested functions. As with other programming languages, we can have also nested functions in Python. One such example is presented as Figure 4.9 with results.

```
File  Edit  Format  Run  Options  Window  Help
# This code is an example for the nested functions usage.
def function_demo_outer ():
    variable1=10
    print ("The variable inside the outer function", variable1)
    def function_demo_inner():
        variable1=20
        print ("The variable inside the inner function", variable1)
# let us call the inner function. See the names of the variable.
    function_demo_inner()
#lets call the outer function
function_demo_outer()
```

```
File  Edit  Shell  Debug  Options  Window  Help
Python 3.7.3 (v3.7.3:ef4ec6ed12, Mar 25 2019, 21:26:53) [MSC v.1916 32 bit (Inte
l)] on win32
Type "help", "copyright", "credits" or "license()" for more information.
>>>
=============== RESTART: E:/Python Playlist/scope_3.py ===============
The variable inside the outer function 10
The variable inside the inner function 20
>>>
```

Figure 4.9   Nested functions.

4.3 Lambda Functions

Lambda functions are a convenient technique to quickly generate short, anonymous functions. They are often referred to as lambda expressions or anonymous functions. When you don't want to use the def keyword to define a whole function, lambda functions can be used. One can see the syntax presented below:

Lambda arguments: <expressions>

One example code is presented below (Figure 4.10). The reader can observe the way the lambda functions are to be used.

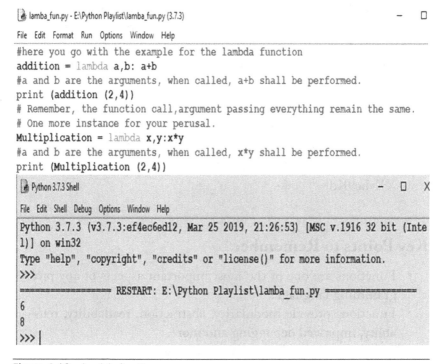

```
lamba_fun.py - E:\Python Playlist\lamba_fun.py (3.7.3)                    –    □

File  Edit  Format  Run  Options  Window  Help
#here you go with the example for the lambda function
addition = lambda a,b: a+b
#a and b are the arguments, when called, a+b shall be performed.
print (addition (2,4))
# Remember, the function call,argument passing everything remain the same.
# One more instance for your perusal.
Multiplication = lambda x,y:x*y
#a and b are the arguments, when called, x*y shall be performed.
print (Multiplication (2,4))
```

```
Python 3.7.3 Shell                                                       –    □    X

File  Edit  Shell  Debug  Options  Window  Help
Python 3.7.3 (v3.7.3:ef4ec6ed12, Mar 25 2019, 21:26:53) [MSC v.1916 32 bit (Inte
l)] on win32
Type "help", "copyright", "credits" or "license()" for more information.
>>>
================ RESTART: E:\Python Playlist\lamba_fun.py ================
6
8
>>> |
```

Figure 4.10 Lambda function.

Can we try using lambda functions with normal functions? Is it possible? The answer is yes, it is very much possible. One can see this from the code presented as Figure 4.11 with results.

```
File  Edit  Format  Run  Options  Window  Help
# Usage of Lambda with the normal function.
# Let us go with a demo!
def function_demo_lambda (x):
     return (lambda a: a*a) (x)

k=10
i=function_demo_lambda(k)
print (i)

>>>
================ RESTART: E:/Python Playlist/lamba_fun1.py ================
100
>>>
```

Figure 4.11 Lambda along with normal functions.

Well, we have reached the end of this chapter. The next chapter will present you with the details of the modules in Python and it will be interesting too.

Readers can watch the following YouTube lectures to gain more understanding.

Python – Functions in Python, definition, default arguments etc.: https://youtu.be/yvNtFDqGlZ4?si=eeHXXA3GZ8I1Bcl9

Python – Nested functions, scope, global statement, lambda functions: https://youtu.be/d6ZHfRGuW4Q?si=gVPEthu5 XEvhe9Kd

Key Points to Remember

- Functions are one of the most important aspects of any programming language.
- Functions provide modularity, abstraction, readability, reusablity, improved debugging and more.
- Python has many built-in functions, while programmers can also define their own functions.
- There is no limit with respect to the number of functions one can define in a program.
- The function block should start with the def keyword.
- One can also write the functions to be interactive.

- Can a function return more than one return value? In Python, it is possible.
- Default assignment provides a default value if a value is not assigned during the function call.
- One can have variable length arguments for the functions in Python.
- Functions can also be nested, meaning that a function can be placed inside another one.
- Lambda functions are a convenient technique to quickly generate short, anonymous functions.

Further Reading

Python Functions – https://cs.stanford.edu/people/nick/py/python-function.html

Python official website – https://www.python.org/

Awesome Python – https://github.com/vinta/awesome-python

5

MODULES IN PYTHON

LEARNING OBJECTIVES

After reading this chapter, readers will have learned about:

- Modules in Python
- The importance of modules
- Math modules
- From and import – must-know
- From, import and as – the "trio"
- Command-line arguments
- Some must-know points.

5.1 Introduction

We discussed the functions in the last chapter and highlighted the various features it offers the programmers. Modules are superior to functions and can be understood once the reader has completed this chapter. Modules are already available Python files (.py files) which one can use, and they can do some predetermined tasks for the programmer, in an easier way. The task could be mathematical or analytical. A module is a file which consist of the Python code. A module can define functions, classes and even variables. Modules are very helpful in grouping pieces of codes together in a file, in a much more logical manner.

DOI: 10.1201/9781032712673-5

5.2 Module Usage and the Creation of Modules

Once the module is available, one can import it to the Python file. One can use the 'import' option to import the modules and can start running the code.

An example will be very helpful for the readers to understand how modules can be imported and used. Figure 5.1 presents a simple example elucidating the usage of modules along with results.

```
module.py - E:/Python Playlist/module.py (3.7.3)

File  Edit  Format  Run  Options  Window  Help
# To find the version of python!
import sys  ──────────  importing a module called sys, which will help in printing
print(sys.prefix)        the version of python

# To print all the environmental variables in one shot.
import os  ──────────  Importing the module OS which can enable printing the details of
for a in os.environ:     environmental variables
    print('Var: ', a, 'Value: ', os.getenv(a))
print("all done")

# This is how you can import the modules.

= RESTART: C:/Users/shriramk/OneDrive - Intel Corporation/Desktop/PythonBook/2.p
y
The version C:\Users\shriramk\AppData\Local\Programs\Python\Python311
Var: ALLUSERSPROFILE Value: C:\ProgramData
Var: APPDATA Value: C:\Users\shriramk\AppData\Roaming
Var: ATERNITY_AGENT_HOME Value: C:\Program Files (x86)\Aternity Information Syst
ems\Agent\
Var: COMMONPROGRAMFILES Value: C:\Program Files\Common Files
Var: COMMONPROGRAMFILES(X86) Value: C:\Program Files (x86)\Common Files
Var: COMMONPROGRAMW6432 Value: C:\Program Files\Common Files
Var: COMPUTERNAME Value: SHRIRAMK-MOBL
Var: COMSPEC Value: C:\WINDOWS\system32\cmd.exe
Var: DRIVERDATA Value: C:\Windows\System32\Drivers\DriverData
Var: FPS_BROWSER_APP_PROFILE_STRING Value: Internet Explorer
Var: FPS_BROWSER_USER_PROFILE_STRING Value: Default
```

Figure 5.1   Importing module – A simple example.

It is time to try something very interesting. Can we create a module ourselves? Yes, readers are presented with an instance where a module is created and used (Figure 5.2).

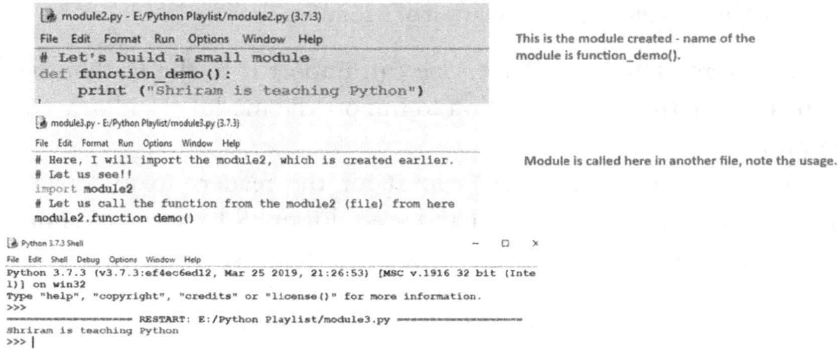

Figure 5.2 Creation of own modules.

5.3 Math Modules

Math is all fun and Python has math modules. It is very easy to use and an instance for generating the square root for the given number with the math module is presented below as Figure 5.3, which includes the result obtained. A simple line import math shall enable the access to the underlying C library functions which makes life easier.

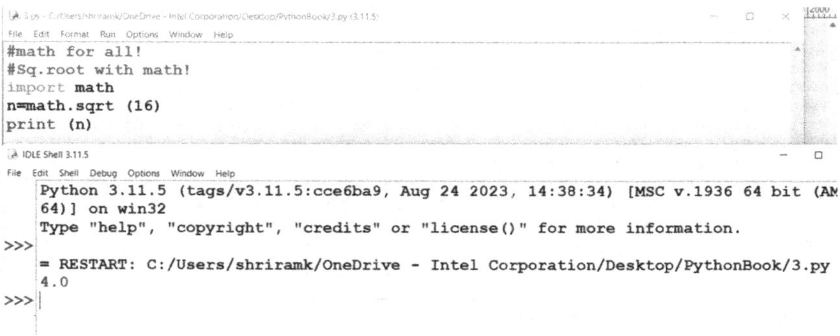

Figure 5.3 Importing math modules.

More math operations are possible to be done with the math module. A sample code covering more math with the support of the math module is presented as Figure 5.4 with results. Readers can see how easy it is to get math implemented with modules.

```
File  Edit  Format  Run  Options  Window  Help
# Can we do math?
# All math in one shot!
import math

# Square Root
n = math.sqrt (4)
print ("Sqrt is",n)

# Ceil returns the smallest integral value greater than number
n = math.ceil (4.87)
print ("ceil is",n)

# floor returns the greatest integral value smaller than number
n = math.floor (4.87)
print ("floored is",n)

#fabs - Returns the absolute value of the given number.
n = math.fabs (5)
print ("fab value is",n)
n = math.fabs (5.222)
print ("fab value is",n)

#factorial
n = math.factorial (4)
print ("factorial is",n)
```

```
File  Edit  Shell  Debug  Options  Window  Help
Python 3.7.3 (v3.7.3:ef4ec6ed12, Mar 25 2019, 21:26:53) [MSC v.1916 32 bit (
1)] on win32
Type "help", "copyright", "credits" or "license()" for more information.
>>>
================= RESTART: E:/Python Playlist/module5.py =================
Sqrt is 2.0
ceil is 5
floored is 4
fab value is 5.0
fab value is 5.222
factorial is 24
>>>
```

Figure 5.4 Easy math with math modules in Python.

More math is presented in the subsequent example presented as Figure 5.5. Readers can see that the copysign, and Greatest Common Divisor (GCD) operations are performed with the usage of math modules seamlessly. From these examples, readers can understand the modules are so helpful and also easy to use.

There are more math functions; readers can try out more such options with math modules.

One can use from and import together, which makes it easier for the programmers. When we import a module, we import everything from it. A couple of examples were just presented. Can someone import

```
File Edit Format Run Options Window Help
# Can we do math?
# All math in one shot!
import math

# copysign - well this is fun
# Function will return the number with value of a, but with the sign of b.
# An instance is helpful as ever.
a = -5
b = 3
# Here, as you see, a is negative, b is positive
print (math.copysign (a,b))

a = 5
b = -3
# Here, as you see, a is negative, b is positive
print (math.copysign (a,b))

# GCD - Let's have fun.
a = 5
b = 10
# Here, as you see, a is negative, b is positive
print (math.gcd (a,b))
```

```
Python 3.7.3 Shell                                          –    □
File Edit Shell Debug Options Window Help
Python 3.7.3 (v3.7.3:ef4ec6ed12, Mar 25 2019, 21:26:53) [MSC v.1916 32 bit (Int
1)] on win32
Type "help", "copyright", "credits" or "license()" for more information.
>>>
================== RESTART: E:/Python Playlist/math1.py ==================
5.0
-5.0
5
```

Figure 5.5 Copysign, GCD with math.

selected stuff from the module? Yes, it can be done. One example is presented below where both from and import are used together. From math, we have imported factorial, as shown in Figure 5.6.

```
module6.py - E:/Python Playlist/module6.py (3.7.3)
File Edit Format Run Options Window Help
# Let us understand the usage of from and import.
from math import factorial
print (factorial (4))
```

```
Python 3.7.3 Shell                                          –    □    ⟩
File Edit Shell Debug Options Window Help
Python 3.7.3 (v3.7.3:ef4ec6ed12, Mar 25 2019, 21:26:53) [MSC v.1916 32 bit (Inte
1)] on win32
Type "help", "copyright", "credits" or "license()" for more information.
>>>
================== RESTART: E:/Python Playlist/module6.py ==================
24
>>> |
```

Figure 5.6 From and Import together.

One can have a look at another example presented below as Figure 5.7 were from and import are used together. This way of programming is very useful to import select modules appropriately.

```
module6.py - E:/Python Playlist/module6.py (3.7.3)

File  Edit  Format  Run  Options  Window  Help

# Let us understand the usage of from and import.
from math import factorial
print (factorial (4))
from math import pi
print (pi)
```

```
Python 3.7.3 Shell                                        —   □   >

File  Edit  Shell  Debug  Options  Window  Help

Python 3.7.3 (v3.7.3:ef4ec6ed12, Mar 25 2019, 21:26:53) [MSC v.1916 32 bit (Inte
1)] on win32
Type "help", "copyright", "credits" or "license()" for more information.
>>>
================= RESTART: E:/Python Playlist/module6.py =================
24
3.141592653589793
>>> |
```

Figure 5.7   From and Import together – another example.

One can use 'as' for aliasing. One instance where 'as' has been used is presented below (Figure 5.8) along with results. In the example, factorial has been used as fact through the aliasing.

```
module7.py - E:\Python Playlist\module7.py (3.7.3)

File  Edit  Format  Run  Options  Window  Help

# Let us understand the usage of from and import.
from math import factorial as fact
print (fact (4))
from math import gcd as Shriram
print (Shriram (5,10))
```

```
Python 3.7.3 (v3.7.3:ef4ec6ed12, Mar 25 2019, 21:26:53) [MSC v.1916 32 bit
1)] on win32
Type "help", "copyright", "credits" or "license()" for more information.
>>>
================= RESTART: E:\Python Playlist\module7.py =================
24
5
>>> |
```

Figure 5.8   'as' with from and import.

5.4 Command-Line Arguments in Python

This is always seen as one of the toughest topics, even in C programming. Many find this difficult to understand and to teach. But this is not so difficult. Readers are introduced to the command line arguments in Python through the simple example presented in Figure 5.9.

```
File  Edit  Format  Run  Options  Window  Help
import sys
x = int (sys.argv[1])
y = int (sys.argv[2])
z = int (sys.argv[3])
total = x + y + z
avg = total/3
print ("Total", total)
print ("Average", avg)
# lets learn the command line arguments
# one should import sys for this to be done.
# Remeber, store this file in appropriate path.
# Else, this wont work!
# Also, Run this as a command.

C:\Users\Subashri\Downloads>python 2.py 1 2 3
Total 6
Average 2.0

C:\Users\Subashri\Downloads>python 2.py 6 8 10
Total 24
Average 8.0
```

Figure 5.9 Command line arguments with Python with results.

Readers have been exposed to more complex topics and we recommend readers to try these out practically to gain more knowledge and understanding.

Readers can watch the following YouTube lectures to gain more understanding:

Modules in Python – https://youtu.be/jcJ3Aq09_tM
Command-line arguments in Python – https://youtu.be/kGb9 czHzzPQ

Key Points to Remember

- Modules are already available Python files (.py files) which one can use. They can carry out some predetermined tasks for the programmer, in an easier way.
- Modules are very helpful in grouping pieces of codes together in a file, in a much more logical manner.
- One can use the 'import' option to import the modules and start running the code.
- Math modules make the life of programmers much easier through various built-in features.
- One can use the from and import functions together, which makes it easier for programmers.
- One can use 'as' for aliasing alongside import.

Further Reading

Python official website – https://www.python.org/
Awesome Python – https://github.com/vinta/awesome-python

NAMESPACE IN PYTHON

LEARNING OBJECTIVES

After reading this chapter, readers will know about the following:

- What a namespace is
- Local, global and built-in namespaces
- How to use calendar
- Time with Python
- Getpass and getuser
- Function redefinition in Python
- Some key points to remember.

6.1 Introduction

A namespace in Python is a container for a collection of identifiers (like class names, variable names, function names, etc.) and the objects (like values, functions or classes) that go along with them. To avoid naming conflicts and improve the modularity and maintainability of your code, namespaces are used to arrange and manage the naming of variables and other objects.

Namespaces in Python prevent the naming ambiguities and enable programmers to use names as they wish. One can understand the usefulness of namespace with an example. Assume that you created two modules, Mod1 and Mod2. Both of the modules may have used the same variable names. In that condition on importing both the modules, there comes uninvited trouble. Yes, it is a pain point.

DOI: 10.1201/9781032712673-6

An example is presented below as Figure 6.1 where two namespaces are present yet having the same variable name – res – used inside both the namespaces. Because the namespace is there, there is no ambiguity, and no error has been created.

```
main.py - E:/Python Playlist/Python Shriram Content/main.py (3.7.3)
File  Edit  Format  Run  Options  Window  Help
# This is main file.
# From here, I shall import name_space_1.py and name_space_2.py
import name_space_1
import name_space_2
res = name_space_1.function_demo(1)
print (res)

res = name_space_2.function_demo(3)
print (res)
```

```
Python 3.7.3 Shell                                          –   □   X
File  Edit  Shell  Debug  Options  Window  Help
Python 3.7.3 (v3.7.3:ef4ec6ed12, Mar 25 2019, 21:26:53) [MSC v.1916 32 bit (Inte
l)] on win32
Type "help", "copyright", "credits" or "license()" for more information.
>>>
========= RESTART: E:/Python Playlist/Python Shriram Content/main.py =========
3
1
>>>
```

Figure 6.1 Namespace example.

6.2 Types of Namespaces

There are several types of namespaces in Python:

- Built-in namespace – The names of all the built-in Python objects, modules and functions are contained in this namespace. It is unnecessary to explicitly import these names because they are always available.
- Global namespace – Names specified at the top level of a script or module are included in this namespace. This is formed upon the import of the module and persists until the Python application ends.

- Local namespace – All the names declared inside a particular function or method are included in this namespace. When the function is invoked, it is formed, and when it ends, it is destroyed.

One can understand the usage of the global, local and built-in namespaces with the code given in Figure 6.2 with results also being presented.

```
# here we go with Global, Local and Built-in Namespace.
# the below function is user defined and is global in scope.
def fun_demo (x): #global namespace.
    print ("Here you go, Global Namespace", x)
    number = 1 # this is local namespace example.
    number = number + 1
    print ("The localnamespace",number)
array_number = [1,2,3,4,5]
print ("The Builtin namespace",sum(array_number))
fun_demo (3+3*2) # function call.
```

```
File  Edit  Shell  Debug  Options  Window  Help

Python 3.7.3 (v3.7.3:ef4ec6ed12, Mar 25 2019, 22:22:05) [MSC v.1916 64 bit (AMD64)] on win32
Type "help", "copyright", "credits" or "license()" for more information.
>>>
======== RESTART: C:\Users\Saihari Shriram\Desktop\Python Files\f3.py ========
The Builtin namespace 15
Here you go, Global Namespace 9
The localnamespace 2
>>>
```

Figure 6.2 Global, local, and built-in namespaces in Python.

It's time for some fun coding now. Readers should certainly enjoy this portion of the learning.

6.3 Calendar

Can we work with the calendar now? Yes, it is fun learning and for someone to use the calendar, the calendar module should have been imported. It is easy to code with the calendar module and the reader is presented with the code where multiple options with calendar module is presented as code (Figure 6.3).

```
File  Edit  Format  Run  Options  Window  Help
# Let us learn the calendar functions here!
import calendar # here is where you import!

# Let us find, if the input year is Leap or not!
# If leap, True shall be returned, else, False.
print (calendar.isleap (2019))
print (calendar.isleap (2020))
print (" ********** *************** ")

# Let us find all the leap years between range (Returns the number)
print ("number of leapyears:",calendar.leapdays(2000, 2019))
print (" ********** *************** ")

# To get to know the day of the week. '0' refers to monday.
print ("Returns the day of the week, 0 for monday",calendar.weekday(2010, 12, 3))
print (" ********** *************** ")

#Returns weekday of first day of the month and number of days in month, for the specified
# year and month.
# 0 refers to Monday.
print (calendar.monthrange(2019, 5))
print (" ********** *************** ")

# To get the calendar printed - Each row represents a week;
print (calendar.monthcalendar(2019, 5))
print (calendar.month (2019, 5))
print (" ********** *************** ")

# This gets the complete calendar for a year.
print (calendar.prcal(2019))
print (calendar.calendar(2019))
```

Figure 6.3   Calendar with Python.

One can now have a look at the results presented below as Figures 6.4 and 6.5, respectively.

```
Python 3.7.3 (v3.7.3:ef4ec6ed12, Mar 25 2019, 22:22:05) [MSC v.1916 64 bit (AMD64)] on win32
Type "help", "copyright", "credits" or "license()" for more information.
>>>
======= RESTART: C:\Users\Saihari Shriram\Desktop\Python Files\cal2.py =======
False
True
********** ***************
number of leapyears: 5
********** ***************
Returns the day of the week, 0 for monday 4
********** ***************
(2, 31)
********** ***************
[[0, 0, 1, 2, 3, 4, 5], [6, 7, 8, 9, 10, 11, 12], [13, 14, 15, 16, 17, 18, 19], [20, 21, 22, 23, 24, 25, 26], [27, 28, 29, 30, 31, 0, 0]]
     May 2019
Mo Tu We Th Fr Sa Su
    1  2  3  4  5
 6  7  8  9 10 11 12
13 14 15 16 17 18 19
20 21 22 23 24 25 26
27 28 29 30 31

********** ***************
```

Figure 6.4   Calendar – results – 1st part.

```
      January            February           March
Mo Tu We Th Fr Sa Su   Mo Tu We Th Fr Sa Su    Mo Tu We Th Fr Sa Su
  1  2  3  4  5  6          1  2  3             1  2  3
  7  8  9 10 11 12 13    4  5  6  7  8  9 10     4  5  6  7  8  9 10
 14 15 16 17 18 19 20   11 12 13 14 15 16 17    11 12 13 14 15 16 17
 21 22 23 24 25 26 27   18 19 20 21 22 23 24    18 19 20 21 22 23 24
 28 29 30 31            25 26 27 28             25 26 27 28 29 30 31


       April               May                June
Mo Tu We Th Fr Sa Su   Mo Tu We Th Fr Sa Su    Mo Tu We Th Fr Sa Su
  1  2  3  4  5  6  7    1  2  3  4  5              1  2
  8  9 10 11 12 13 14    6  7  8  9 10 11 12     3  4  5  6  7  8  9
 15 16 17 18 19 20 21   13 14 15 16 17 18 19    10 11 12 13 14 15 16
 22 23 24 25 26 27 28   20 21 22 23 24 25 26    17 18 19 20 21 22 23
 29 30                  27 28 29 30 31          24 25 26 27 28 29 30


       July               August             September
Mo Tu We Th Fr Sa Su   Mo Tu We Th Fr Sa Su    Mo Tu We Th Fr Sa Su
  1  2  3  4  5  6  7    1  2  3  4                    1
  8  9 10 11 12 13 14    5  6  7  8  9 10 11     2  3  4  5  6  7  8
 15 16 17 18 19 20 21   12 13 14 15 16 17 18     9 10 11 12 13 14 15
 22 23 24 25 26 27 28   19 20 21 22 23 24 25    16 17 18 19 20 21 22
 29 30 31               26 27 28 29 30 31       23 24 25 26 27 28 29
                        30


      October            November           December
Mo Tu We Th Fr Sa Su   Mo Tu We Th Fr Sa Su    Mo Tu We Th Fr Sa Su
  1  2  3  4  5  6          1  2  3                    1
  7  8  9 10 11 12 13    4  5  6  7  8  9 10     2  3  4  5  6  7  8
 14 15 16 17 18 19 20   11 12 13 14 15 16 17     9 10 11 12 13 14 15
 21 22 23 24 25 26 27   18 19 20 21 22 23 24    16 17 18 19 20 21 22
 28 29 30 31            25 26 27 28 29 30       23 24 25 26 27 28 29
```

Figure 6.5   Calendar – results – 2nd part.

6.4 It's Time to Learn About the Time Module

The time module provides time-related functions, and there are many built-in options. One can use all of them and it is a very easy-to-use module. Readers are presented with an example code where a time module with gmtime and localtime options is presented. Results are also presented for better understanding (Figure 6.6).

```
File    Edit    Format    Run    Options    Window    Help
# Let us learn the time related functions here.
import time # here is where you import!

# time.asctime - Returns the current time.
time_now = time.asctime (time.localtime(time.time()))
print ("the time", time_now)
time_now = time.asctime (time.gmtime(time.time()))
print ("the time", time_now)
# gmtime() or localtime() can be used.
```

```
======= RESTART: C:\Users\Saihari Shriram\Desktop\Python Files\time.py :
the time Tue May 14 19:29:11 2019
the time Tue May 14 13:59:11 2019
>>>
```

Figure 6.6   Time module in Python.

It is important to learn the getpass and is explained subsequently.

6.5 Getpass with Python

Passwords and other sensitive data can be safely entered by the user into Python using the getpass module, which does not show the input on the screen. When you wish to write scripts or command line programs that need sensitive data entry or user authentication, this can be quite helpful. One easy way to hide user input is to utilize the getpass module. Readers are requested to try this below piece of code to understand how getpass work (Figure 6.7).

```
4.py - C:/Users/shriramk/OneDrive - Intel Corporation/Desktop/PythonBook/4.py (3.11.5)        —    □    ×
File  Edit  Format  Run  Options  Window  Help
# We are using the getpass module and should be imported first
import getpass
key = getpass.getpass (prompt='Enter the password')
if key == 'sachin':
    print("Python is fun")
else:
    print("You cant breach the password security")
```

Figure 6.7   'getpass' in Python.

6.6 Getuser in Python

If one wants to know the username, it is easy to know with getuser. One can refer to the code and output presented with Figure 6.8.

Figure 6.8 'getuser' in Python.

It is time to understand the function redefinition possibility with Python.

6.7 Function Redefinition in Python

Can we think of a scenario where a function can be redefined? This is an interesting scenario. Can this be done with Python? Yes, it is possible, and Python enables the redefinition of a variable and to redefine a function. An example will make it easy for readers to grasp the concept and the same is presented as Figure 6.9.

Readers can watch the following YouTube lectures to gain more understanding:

Namespace in Python – https://youtu.be/-sZI9t1FKhg?si= OTQkdDu_j-iGWil-

Python – getuser, getpass, calendar, time, function redefinition – https://youtu.be/qHWpLKCR4K8?si=GhUs0mcF2cE9qXrY

```
# Here, we go with the function and variable redefinition example.
# First Definition.
def fun_demo (x):
    x = x * 2
    print ("The number is",x)
fun_demo (3+3*2) # function call.
# Second Definition
def fun_demo (x):
    x = x - 2
    print ("The number is",x)
fun_demo (3+3+2) # function call.
# Redefining a variable
variable_1 = 10
print ("The initial assignment is", variable_1)
variable_1 = "Hello, World"
print ("Altered assignment is", variable_1)
```

```
Python 3.7.3 (v3.7.3:ef4ec6ed12, Mar 25 2019, 22:22:05) [MSC v.1916 64 bit (AMD64)] on win32
Type "help", "copyright", "credits" or "license()" for more information.
>>>

======= RESTART: C:/Users/Saihari Shriram/Desktop/Python Files/f10.py =======
The number is 18
The number is 6
The initial assignment is 10
Altered assignment is Hello, World
>>>
```

Figure 6.9   Function and variable redefinition example with results.

Key Points to Remember

- A namespace in Python is a container for a collection of identifiers.
- To avoid naming conflicts and improve the modularity and maintainability of your code, namespaces are used to arrange and manage the naming of variables and other objects.
- In a built-in namespace, the names of all the built-in Python objects, modules and functions are contained in this namespace. It is not necessary to explicitly import these names because they are always available.
- In a global namespace, names specified at the top level of a script or module are included in this namespace. This is formed following the import of the module and persists until the Python application ends.

- When it comes to a local namespace, all the names declared inside a particular function or method are included in this namespace. When the function is invoked, it is formed, and when it ends, it is destroyed.
- The calendar module provides numerous features related to calendar and can be imported and used.
- The time module provides time-related functions, and many built-in options are there.
- If one wants to know the username, it is easy to know with the getuser module.
- Passwords and other sensitive data can be safely entered by the user into Python using the getpass module, which does not show the input on the screen
- Python enables to redefine a variable and to redefine a function.

Further Reading

Python official website – https://www.python.org/
Awesome Python – https://github.com/vinta/awesome-python

7

STRINGS – STRIKE THE RIGHT CHORDS

LEARNING OBJECTIVES

After reading this chapter, the readers will have learned about:

- The basics of strings
- Indexing with strings
- String traversal operation
- String concatenation
- Appending operations with string
- Ignoring the escape sequences
- Built-in string functions
- Some interesting facts and points to remember.

7.1 Introduction

Python's string-handling capabilities make it a versatile language for working with textual data, from basic string manipulation to more advanced text-processing tasks. In Python, a string is a sequence of characters, and is one of the fundamental data types used to represent and manipulate text. Strings are used to store and work with textual data, such as words, sentences or any combination of characters. Strings are enclosed in either single quotes (') or double quotes ("), and they can also be enclosed in triple-quotes (''' or """) for multiline text. This chapter shall present the readers with all possible string operations.

DOI: 10.1201/9781032712673-7

7.2 String Traversal and Other String Operations

Readers are presented with a simple Python code where string traversal is performed. One can see that the string "Sachin_Tendulkar" is the chosen string. The code and the results are presented for the string traversal as Figure 7.1. String traversal, often referred to as "iterating through a string" or "string iteration," involves systematically processing each character in a string one by one. In Python, this is typically done using a loop, such as a for loop, to access and work with each character in the string sequentially.

```
File  Edit  Format  Run  Options  Window  Help
# Here, We shall learn the string traversal!
# Remember, we need to have the index! Else, gone!

string = "Sachin_Tendulkar"
index = 0 # See, this is index!
print ("Here you go, the characters from the string")
for i in string: # here, we use for, it loops.
     print (i)
index = index + 1
```

```
Python 3.7.3 (v3.7.3:ef4ec6ed12, Mar 25 2019, 21:26:53) [MSC v.1916 32 bit (Inte
l)] on win32
Type "help", "copyright", "credits" or "license()" for more information.
>>>
============== RESTART: F:/Python Playlist/Shriram/str1.py ==============
Here you go, the characters from the string
S
a
c
h
i
n
_
T
e
n
d
u
l
k
a
r
>>>
```

Figure 7.1   The string traversal.

String concatenation is the process of combining (joining or merging) two or more strings into a single, longer string. In Python you can concatenate strings with ease. The code and the results for the string concatenation operation is presented as Figure 7.2. Readers can try this out practically.

```
File  Edit  Format  Run  Options  Window  Help
# String Concatenation - A Quick View!!
String_Firsthalf = "Sachin"
String_Secondhalf = "Tendulkar"
String = String_Firsthalf + String_Secondhalf
print ("Here you go", String)

Python 3.7.3 (v3.7.3:ef4ec6ed12, Mar 25 2019, 21:26:53) [MSC v.1916 32 bit (Inte
1)] on win32
Type "help", "copyright", "credits" or "license()" for more information.
>>>
=============== RESTART: F:/Python Playlist/Shriram/str2.py ===============
Here you go SachinTendulkar
>>> |
```

Figure 7.2   The string concatenation.

It is very easy to append strings with more content. One such example is presented as Figure 7.3 where results are also presented. One can observe that is very easy to carry out the appending operation.

```
File  Edit  Format  Run  Options  Window  Help
# Append String
String_First = "Sachin"
String_Append = print ("Enter the string to be appended")
String_First += "Tendulkar is the greatest of cricketers"
print (String_First)

Python 3.7.3 (v3.7.3:ef4ec6ed12, Mar 25 2019, 21:26:53) [MSC v.1916 32 bit (Inte
1)] on win32
Type "help", "copyright", "credits" or "license()" for more information.
>>>
=============== RESTART: F:/Python Playlist/Shriram/str3.py ===============
Enter the string to be appended
SachinTendulkar is the greatest of cricketers
```

Figure 7.3   The string appending operation.

Can we print a string multiple times with ease? Yes, it is possible and * can be used to accomplish the task. One can have closer look at the code and result presented as Figure 7.4.

```
# can we print a string multiple time - in one shot!
# Easy do it with * operator
string_example = "\n Sachin Tendulkar"
print (string_example * 4)
```

```
Python 3.7.3 (v3.7.3:ef4ec6ed12, Mar 25 2019, 21:26:53) [MSC v.1916 32 bit (Inte
l)] on win32
Type "help", "copyright", "credits" or "license()" for more information.
>>>
================ RESTART: F:/Python Playlist/Shriram/str4.py ================

Sachin Tendulkar
Sachin Tendulkar
Sachin Tendulkar
Sachin Tendulkar
```

Figure 7.4   Print string multiple times.

Can the programmer ignore the escape sequence? Yes, it is very much possible with Python and a simple code with results is presented as Figure 7.5. One can visualize from the results that the escape sequence is ignored through the second print statement.

```
File  Edit  Format  Run  Options  Window  Help
# Let's igonore the escape sequence.
print ("\n Sachin Tendulkar")
print (r"\n Sachin Tendulkar")

================ RESTART: F:/Python Playlist/Shriram/str4.py ================

Sachin Tendulkar
\n Sachin Tendulkar
>>> |
```

Figure 7.5   Ignore escape sequence.

7.3 Built-in String Functions – A Quick Lesson

There are multiple built-in string functions presented in Python. This section explains such built-in string functions with examples.

One can see the capitalize function, which is used in the code presented as Figure 7.6. On running the code, the results arrive with the first character being capitalized.

```
File  Edit  Format  Run  Options  Window  Help
# Inbuit String Functions - A quick overview
# Capitalize Function
str_demo = "shriram"
print (str_demo.capitalize())
str_demo = "sachin"
print (str_demo.capitalize())
str_demo = "tendulkar"
print (str_demo.capitalize())
```

```
Python 3.7.3 Shell                                          -  □
File  Edit  Shell  Debug  Options  Window  Help
Python 3.7.3 (v3.7.3:ef4ec6ed12, Mar 25 2019, 21:26:53) [MSC v.1916 32 bit (I:
1)] on win32
Type "help", "copyright", "credits" or "license()" for more information.
>>>
=============== RESTART: F:/Python Playlist/Shriram/str5.py ===============
Shriram
Sachin
Tendulkar
>>>
```

Figure 7.6   'capitalize' – String function.

The center() method in Python is a built-in string method that is used to center-align a string within a specified width. It's often used for formatting text to ensure that it appears centered when displayed. One such example is presented below where one can see the way the output appears in a much more readable format (Figure 7.7).

```
str6.py - F:/Python Playlist/Shriram/str6.py (3.7.3)
File  Edit  Format  Run  Options  Window  Help
# Inbuit String Functions - A quick overview
# center Function
str_demo = "Sachin"
print(str_demo.center(20, '*'))
```

```
Python 3.7.3 Shell                                          -  □
File  Edit  Shell  Debug  Options  Window  Help
Python 3.7.3 (v3.7.3:ef4ec6ed12, Mar 25 2019, 21:26:53) [MSC v.1916 32 bit (Int
1)] on win32
Type "help", "copyright", "credits" or "license()" for more information.
>>>
=============== RESTART: F:/Python Playlist/Shriram/str6.py ===============
*******Sachin*******
>>>
```

Figure 7.7   'center' method.

The count is the next built-in function to be covered. To find the number of times a particular substring or element appears in a string, list, or other iterable, use Python's built-in count() function, which is also available for lists and other sequences. It's a practical method for handling basic counting chores without requiring the creation of unique loops or manual sequence iteration. A code and results are presented as Figure 7.8 for the readers to understand things better.

```
File Edit Format Run Options Window Help
# Inbuit String Functions - A quick overview
# Counts number of times a particular string appears in a bigger string
str_demo = "SachinTendulkarSachinTendulkarSachinTendulkar"
test="Sachin"
print (str_demo.count(test,0,len(str_demo)))

str_demo = "SachinTendulkarSachinTendulkarSachinTendulkar"
test="Sachin"
print (str_demo.count(test,10,len(str_demo)))
```
```
File Edit Shell Debug Options Window Help
Python 3.7.3 (v3.7.3:ef4ec6ed12, Mar 25 2019, 21:26:53) [MSC v.1916 32 bit (Int
l)] on win32
Type "help", "copyright", "credits" or "license()" for more information.
>>>
================ RESTART: F:/Python Playlist/Shriram/str6.py ================
3
2
>>>
```

Figure 7.8 'count' method.

A built-in string method in Python called endswith() is used to determine whether a given string ends with a given suffix, or substring. If the string ends with the designated suffix, it returns True; if not, it returns False. Yes, it is also possible, and a sample code is presented in Figure 7.9.

```
File Edit Format Run Options Window Help
# Inbuit String Functions - A quick overview
# endswith checks if a string ends with a particular sequence!
str_demo = "Sachin Tendulkar"
test="kar"
print (str_demo.endswith(test,0,len(str_demo)))

str_demo = "Sachin Tendulkar"
test="kamb"
print (str_demo.endswith(test,0,len(str_demo)))
```

```
File Edit Shell Debug Options Window Help
Python 3.7.3 (v3.7.3:ef4ec6ed12, Mar 25 2019, 21:26:53) [MSC v.1916 32 bit (Inte
1)] on win32
Type "help", "copyright", "credits" or "license()" for more information.
>>>
=============== RESTART: F:/Python Playlist/Shriram/str7.py ===============
True
False
>>>
```

Figure 7.9 'endswith' method.

Next, we can find if a string is present in another string! Will return the position i.e., the character position if present. If not present, -1 will be returned. Find is the method used to get this task done. A sample code and results are presented as Figure 7.10.

```
# Inbuit String Functions - A quick overview
# find- checks if a string has another string!
str_demo = "Sachin Tendulkar"
test="kar"
print (str_demo.find(test,0,len(str_demo)))

str_demo = "Sachin Tendulkar"
test="kamb"
print (str_demo.find(test,0,len(str_demo)))
```

```
Python 3.7.3 (v3.7.3:ef4ec6ed12, Mar 25 2019, 21:26:53) [MSC v.1916 32 bit (Inte
1)] on win32
Type "help", "copyright", "credits" or "license()" for more information.
>>>
=============== RESTART: F:/Python Playlist/Shriram/str8.py ===============
13
-1
>>>
```

Figure 7.10 'find' method.

A built-in string method in Python called isalnum() can be used to determine whether every character in a given string is an alphanumeric character. A character that is either a letter (a to z or A to Z) or a numeral (0 to 9) is known as an alphanumeric character. If the string contains any non-alphanumeric characters, the isalnum() method returns False. Otherwise, it returns True if all of the characters in the string are alphanumeric. A simple code is presented as Figure 7.11 with results for enhanced understanding.

```
File Edit Format Run Options Window Help
str_demo = "Sachin Tendulkar 200 Not out"
print (str_demo.isalnum())

str_demo = "SachinTendulkar200Notout"
print (str_demo.isalnum())
```

```
File Edit Shell Debug Options Window Help
Python 3.7.3 (v3.7.3:ef4ec6ed12, Mar 25 2019, 21:26:53) [MSC v.1916 32 bit (Inte
l)] on win32
Type "help", "copyright", "credits" or "license()" for more information.
>>>
=============== RESTART: F:/Python Playlist/Shriram/str9.py ===============
False
True
>>>
```

Figure 7.11   'isalnum()' method.

When you need to confirm that a string is made up just of alphabetic characters – such as the letters of a word or name – the isalpha() method comes in rather helpful. It can be applied to a variety of Python programs for tasks, including filtering, input checking and data validation. A sample code is presented as Figure 7.12 where the isalpha() method is used.

```
str_demo = "Sachin Tendulkar 200 Not out"
print (str_demo.isalpha())

str_demo = "SachinTendulkar200Notout"
print (str_demo.isalpha())

str_demo = "SachinTendulkarNotout"
print (str_demo.isalpha())
```

File Edit Shell Debug Options Window Help

```
Python 3.7.3 (v3.7.3:ef4ec6ed12, Mar 25 2019, 21:26:53) [MSC v.1916 3
1)] on win32
Type "help", "copyright", "credits" or "license()" for more informatic
>>>
================ RESTART: F:/Python Playlist/Shriram/str10.py =======
False
False
True
\ \ \
```

Figure 7.12 'isalnum()' method.

Readers can watch the following YouTube lectures to gain more understanding:

Python – String Operations – Complete Analysis – https://youtu.be/-1k7ROwQMws?si=bgHBVoc4a78TP1sH

Key Points to Remember

- String traversal, string concatenation and string-appending operations can be done with ease in Python.
- There are multiple built-in string functions presented in Python.
- The center() method in Python is a built-in string method that is used to center-align a string within a specified width.
- To find the number of times a particular substring or element appears in a string, list or other iterable, one can use Python's built-in count() function.
- A built-in string method in Python called endswith() is used to determine whether a given string ends with a given suffix, or substring.

- A built-in string method in Python called isalnum() can be used to determine whether every character in a given string is an alphanumeric character.
- When you need to confirm that a string is made up just of alphabetic characters – such as the letters of a word or name – the isalpha() method can be used.

Further Reading

Python official website – https://www.python.org/
Awesome Python – https://github.com/vinta/awesome-python

8

PYTHON AND FILES

LEARNING OBJECTIVES

After reading this chapter, readers will be aware of:

- File fundamentals
- How to open a file
- Methods to use read, readline and readlines
- Renaming files
- The file removal process
- Some very important points to remember.

8.1 Introduction

You can work with files on your computer using file operations in Python. You can create and delete files, read from, and write to files, and do a lot of other things. This chapter deals with the various file operations using examples. Readers are encouraged to try these out practically to gain a better understanding.

8.2 Files in Python

A file is a grouping of data or information kept on a hard disk, solid-state drive, or other type of storage medium in a computer. Different kinds of data, such as text, pictures, audio, video, applications, configuration settings and more, can be found in files. An essential component of computer systems, files are used to store and organize data in an accessible and orderly way.

DOI: 10.1201/9781032712673-8

83

8.2.1 Opening a File

The open() method in Python is used to open files for reading, writing and adding data to a file, among other file actions. You can utilize the file object that is returned by the open() function to carry out file-related tasks. The syntax for the open() method is presented below with an instance where the same used to open a file with wb mode.

file = open(file_path, mode)
⇩
fp = open("test.txt", "wb")

One should understand that,

file_path is the path to open the file. It can be either a relative or an absolute file path.

Mode specifies the mode you want to open the file. It can be any one of the following:

- 'r': Read mode, which is the default mode.
- 'w': Write mode and the file will be opened for the write process. If the file already exists, it will be truncated (cleared). If not, a new file will be created.
- 'a': Append mode gets the file opened for writing, but data is appended to the end of the file instead of overwriting its contents. If the file doesn't exist, this mode will create a new file.
- 'b': Binary mode is normally used along with other modes to open files in binary mode (e.g., 'rb' for reading a binary file, 'wb' for writing a binary file).
- 't': Text mode and is used to open files in text mode (e.g., 'rt' for reading a text file, 'wt' for writing a text file).

To free up system resources, it's crucial to use the close() method to end the file after you're finished with it. Nevertheless, using the with statement to have the file automatically close when you leave the block is a more advised strategy.

A sample code is presented below as Figure 8.1 where a file is opened, and results are displayed.

```
File Edit Format Run Options Window Help
# Open the file for reading
with open("data_test.txt", "r") as file:
    # Read file contents.
    data = file.read()

# We print it now.
print(data)
```

```
IDLE Shell 3.11.5                                              —    □    ×
File Edit Shell Debug Options Window Help
    Python 3.11.5 (tags/v3.11.5:cce6ba9, Aug 24 2023, 14:38:34) [MSC v.1936 64 b
    it (AMD64)] on win32
    Type "help", "copyright", "credits" or "license()" for more information.
>>>
    Sachin Tendulkar
    is the
    God
    of Cricket
```

Figure 8.1 'open()' operation with Python.

One can also use readline(), readlines() and read(). The file data_test.txt is already created and it has the content as presented in Figure 8.2.

Figure 8.2 File 'data_test.txt' content.

Figure 8.3 presents code with results where read(), readline(), readlines() are used. One can understand the differences easily on seeing the execution results.

Can we rename a file through a Python code? Yes, it is possible.

The method rename enables renaming a file with ease. It needs the current name and proposed name as input. A code snippet is presented along with execution result as Figure 8.4. But one must remember that the os module must be imported before trying this renaming action. Before the execution of the code, the file name was old_file_name; on execution, it is renamed as new_file_name. The same can be observed from Figure 8.4.

```
File  Edit  Format  Run  Options  Window  Help
# This read and readline helps in reading he string!
# Reading options - let us understand.
#To open and to read one line from the file:
fp = open("file_1.txt", "r")
print (fp.readline())
print (fp.readline())
print (fp.readline())
print ("***********")

#To open and to read list of lines:
fp = open("file_1.txt", "r")
print (fp.readlines())
print ("***********")

#Can we write some content into a file?
fp = open("file_2.txt","w")
fp.write("Sachin_Tendulkar_is_Greatest")
fp.close()

#After writing the content, we should read.
fp = open("file_2.txt", "r")
print (fp.readline())
print ("***********")
```

```
File  Edit  Shell  Debug  Options  Window  Help
Python 3.6.5 (v3.6.5:f59c0932b4, Mar 28 2018, 17:00:18) [MSC v.1900 64 bit (AMD6
4)] on win32
Type "copyright", "credits" or "license()" for more information.
>>>
================ RESTART: F:/Python Playlist/Shriram/file2.py ================
Sachin_Tendulkar

Brian_Lara

Kapil_Dev

**********
['Sachin_Tendulkar\n', 'Brian_Lara\n', 'Kapil_Dev \n', 'MS Dhoni \n', 'Rahul_Dra
vid \n', 'Sourav_Ganguly ']
**********
Sachin_Tendulkar_is_Greatest
**********
```

Figure 8.3 'read()', 'readline()', 'readlines()' code and results.

```
File  Edit  Format  Run  Options  Window  Help
# Rename shall enable renaming a file with ease.
# It needs the current name and proposed name as input.
# Let us see a demo!
# But, remember, we should import the OS module!!
import os
os.rename("old_file_name.txt", "new_file_name.txt")
```

Figure 8.4 Renaming a file.

Can someone remove a file through a Python code? Yes, it can be done. The remove method should be used, where one has to specify the name of the file to be removed. On execution, the file will be removed. One can understand the same from the code presented below along with the results shown as Figure 8.5. But one must remember that the os module must be imported before trying removal of a file.

SHRIRAM K V (F:)	test	19-05-2019 20:47	Text Document	0 KB
DST Proposal	write	19-05-2019 20:18	Text Document	1 KB
Genesys Hack	file_2	19-05-2019 20:58	Text Document	1 KB
Others	file3	19-05-2019 21:57	Python File	1 KB
	new_file_name	19-05-2019 20:18	Text Document	1 KB

file4.py - F:/Python Playlist/Shriram/file4.py (3.7.3)

File Edit Format Run Options Window Help

```
# Can we remove a file for ever?
import os
os.remove ("new_file_name.txt")
```

SHRIRAM K V (F:)	write	19-05-2019 20:18	Text Document	1 KB
DST Proposal	file_2	19-05-2019 20:58	Text Document	1 KB
Genesys Hack	file3	19-05-2019 21:57	Python File	1 KB
Others	file4	19-05-2019 22:01	Python File	1 KB

Figure 8.5 Removal of a file.

One could observe that the file new_file_name was present previously and, after execution, it is removed permanently.

Readers can watch the following YouTube lectures to gain more understanding:

- Python – File operations in Python – https://youtu.be/ rwFbHVLCSYU?si=jRBLg711j-qvPar1

Key Points to Remember

- The open() method in Python is used to open files for reading, writing and adding data to a file.
- One can open the file in different modes such as read mode, write mode, append mode, binary mode and text mode.
- A file, once opened, should also be closed.

- read(), readline(), readlines() are different file access methods supported in Python.
- rename method can enable the users to rename files easily.
- remove method can enable the users to remove the files.
- Most of the file access methods require the import module to be used.

Further Reading

Python official website – https://www.python.org/
Awesome Python – https://github.com/vinta/awesome-python

9

PYTHON AND DIRECTORIES

LEARNING OBJECTIVES

After reading this chapter, readers will be aware of:

• Complete directory operations with code.

9.1 Introduction

In the file system of your computer, directories are called folders or directories. Files of all kinds, including text, graphic and Python programs, are stored and arranged using them. Directories are essential for managing and arranging the files and resources in your project. The os module in Python can be used to work with directories (or the pathlib module for a more current and object-oriented approach). This chapter presents the readers with typical Python activities that can be carried out with directories.

9.2 Directory Creation

We can do all what we could do with Linux commands in Python as well. We can create a directory first. We need the mkdir method for the same. One has to import the os module for this task to be accomplished.

A simple example is presented to the readers for understanding the usage of mkdir method. Results are also presented as Figure 9.1, along with results. One could see the director Shriram_Created_Dir has been newly created on the execution of the file using the mkdir method.

DOI: 10.1201/9781032712673-9

file5.py - F:/Python Playlist/Shriram/file5.py (3.6.5)

File   Edit   Format   Run   Options   Window   Help

```
import os
os.mkdir("Shriram_Created_Dir")
```

←   ∨   ↑   □   > SHRIRAM K V (F:) > Python Playlist > Shriram

Name	Date modified	Type	Size
file_1	19-05-2019 20:57	Text Document	1 KB
file1	19-05-2019 20:40	Python File	1 KB
file2	19-05-2019 20:58	Python File	1 KB
str1	19-05-2019 08:28	Python File	1 KB
str2	19-05-2019 08:36	Python File	1 KB
str3	19-05-2019 08:45	Python File	1 KB
str4	19-05-2019 11:21	Python File	1 KB
str5	19-05-2019 11:38	Python File	1 KB
str6	19-05-2019 12:43	Python File	1 KB
str7	19-05-2019 12:50	Python File	1 KB
str8	19-05-2019 12:57	Python File	1 KB
str9	19-05-2019 14:29	Python File	1 KB
str10	19-05-2019 14:47	Python File	1 KB
test	19-05-2019 20:47	Text Document	0 KB
write	19-05-2019 20:18	Text Document	1 KB
file_2	19-05-2019 20:58	Text Document	1 KB
file3	19-05-2019 21:57	Python File	1 KB
file4	19-05-2019 22:01	Python File	1 KB
file5	19-05-2019 22:13	Python File	1 KB
Shriram_Created_Dir	19-05-2019 22:13	File folder	

Quick access
This PC
  3D Objects
  Desktop
  Documents
  Downloads
  Music
  Pictures
  Videos
  Windows Here (C:)
  Data_Education (D:)
  SHRIRAM K V (F:)
SHRIRAM K V (F:)
  DST Proposal
  Genesys Hack
  Others
  Presentation @ PA College
  Python Playlist

Figure 9.1   'mkdir' with Python.

Can someone check the current working directory with simple Python code? This is like the pwd command in Linux. One could see the way getcwd is used in the code shown as Figure 9.2, where the current working directory is presented in the result.

file5.py - F:/Python Playlist/Shriram/file5.py (3.6.5)

File   Edit   Format   Run   Options   Window   Help

```
import os
print (os.getcwd())
```

```
Python 3.6.5 (v3.6.5:f59c0932b4, Mar 28 2018, 17:00:18) [MSC v.1900 64 bit (AMD
4)] on win32
Type "copyright", "credits" or "license()" for more information.
>>>
=============== RESTART: F:/Python Playlist/Shriram/file5.py ===============
>>>
=============== RESTART: F:/Python Playlist/Shriram/file5.py ===============
F:\Python Playlist\Shriram
>>>
```

Figure 9.2   'getcwd' with Python.

One can check if a directory is present using the piece of code presented in Figure 9.3. This will get the verification done and the result will be presented appropriately.

```
9.py - C:/Users/shriramk/OneDrive - Intel Corporation/Desktop/PythonBook/9.py (3.11.5)    □    ×
File  Edit  Format  Run  Options  Window  Help
import os
# Using os
if os.path.exists("new_directory"):
    print("Directory exists")
else:
    print("Directory does not exist")
```

```
IDLE Shell 3.11.5    □    ×
File  Edit  Shell  Debug  Options  Window  Help
    Python 3.11.5 (tags/v3.11.5:cce6ba9, Aug 24 2023, 14:38:34) [MSC v.1936 64 bit (
    AMD64)] on win32
    Type "help", "copyright", "credits" or "license()" for more information.
>>>
    = RESTART: C:/Users/shriramk/

    Directory does not exist
>>>
```

Figure 9.3 Checking if a directory exists.

One can also list contents of a particular directory. A simple example is presented below as Figure 9.4. Readers can try this out in a practical setting and observe the results. The name of the directory should be properly presented for the code to run.

```
File  Edit  Format  Run  Options  Window  Help
import os
# Using os
files = os.listdir("new_directory")
```

Figure 9.4 Listing directory contents.

If changing the directory is required, one can easily accomplish the same with below piece of code snippet presented as Figure 9.5. One

```
11.py - C:/Users/shriramk/OneDrive - Intel Corporation/Desktop/PythonBook/11.py (3.11.5)
File  Edit  Format  Run  Options  Window  Help
import os
os.chdir("new_directory")
```

Figure 9.5 Change directory with 'chdir' method.

should present the name of the directory appropriately; else the code may not work as expected.

Readers can watch the following YouTube lectures to gain more understanding:

Python directory operations – https://youtu.be/SmjpZV-6BCY

Key Points to Remember

- In the file system of your computer, directories are called folders or directories.
- Files of all kinds, including text, graphic, and Python programs, are stored and arranged using them.
- Directories are essential for managing and arranging the files and resources in your project.
- The os module in Python can be used to work with directories.
- The mkdir method can be used to create a new directory.
- The getcwd method shall be helpful in getting the current working directory.
- One can change directory easily with the chdir method.
- It is easy to test if a directory is present through exists method.

Further Reading

Python official website – https://www.python.org/
Awesome Python – https://github.com/vinta/awesome-python

10

DATA STRUCTURES IN PYTHON

LEARNING OBJECTIVES

After reading through this chapter, reader shall be able to understand the following:

- Arrays and lists and their operations
- Stack in Python
- Queue in Python
- Enumerate
- Zip and dictionaries
- Some key points to remember.

10.1 Introduction

Let us ask a simple question. What does the word structure mean? Structured means organized. Now, the question is: what is a data structure? The answer is simple, structured data, that is, organized data. To make it clear, one can say, "A data structure is a format for storing the data in an organized manner." The readers could even be surprised to know that they have already been familiar with data structures. If terms such as array, record or file are familiar to the reader, then data structure is also familiar.

The next question in the minds of the readers would be: why should we organize the data or why do we need data structures? This is a valid question and here is the explanation. Assume that you have a rack with lot of books dealing with different subjects like Computer

DOI: 10.1201/9781032712673-10

Science, Biology and Physics. The books are not organized and randomly piled up. One can refer to Figure 10.1 to understand what is being portrayed.

Figure 10.1   An unorganized rack of books.

It is very easy to interpret that picking out one book on a particular topic from the unorganized rack is a tough task and a nightmare if the table is huge with a greater number of books in place. Coming to the next scenario, assume a rack which is neatly organized with books properly sectioned out, as shown in Figure 10.2. The question now is: how difficult would it be to spot a book from this organized rack? It

Figure 10.2   An organized rack.

would not take much time and should be very easy. This is the difference readers should understand.

Coming back to computer science, data structures are all about organizing the data, managing the same and storing the same. This shall enable efficient access with an increased ease of access. Let us get the understanding better with more discussion.

10.1.1 Why Do We Need Data Structure?

Most of the interviews, examinations and discussions will certainly have this question. Yes, it is such an important question to be answered. This understanding shall inculcate the interest in the reader to learn the subject and concepts deeper. Data structure is a method/technique for storing and organizing the information in a computing machine. Since it is all organized and well maintained, storage is properly taken care of and the data being searched for can be retrieved much easily and fast, hence effectively increasing the productivity. There is no single type of data structure that the reader is going to be introduced with. There are many types of classifications, and each of these is unique. Data structures are generally classified as either primitive or non-primitive, and one can choose the appropriate option based on the requirements and suitability.

Experienced programmers shall agree to this point that the choice of the data structure chosen and implemented can really make a lot of difference between a program which runs very slow or very fast, preferably in a few seconds. Hence, data structures are important to organize the data and to make sure that retrieval happens fast when they are searched for data.

10.2 Arrays – The Basic Data Structure

An array is a collection of memory location. It is a pre-defined data structure in all programming languages. This is the basic and foremost data structure. Consider an ice tray in the Figure 10.3. It has six empty spaces, so it can hold six ice cubes. The spaces can be left unused, but it cannot more than six ice cubes. The same is the case with arrays. The memory locations cannot be split from each other, so if there is some empty space, it just goes to waste. In addition, arrays cannot be

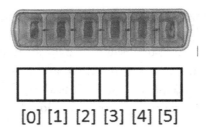

[0] [1] [2] [3] [4] [5]

Figure 10.3   Ice cube tray and a visual representation of an array.

interchanged. For example, an ice tray can hold only ice cubes and an egg tray can have only eggs. An array is a collection of variables of the same type. It cannot hold variables of different types. All the blocks in an array are of same size, as it holds only the same type of variables. A visual representation of an array is also shown in Figure 10.3.

10.2.1 Declaration of Arrays

The position of each memory space is indicated by a number. This is called the index or subscript. The memory address of the first location is stored alone in the variable declaration, while others are calculated relatively. Say, 'a' is the name of the array. Then, a[3] = address of a[0] + 3. While declaration, the address of a[0], that is the starting address of the array, will be associated with the variables name 'a' in the internal symbol table. Arrays can also be declared using pointers in C or C++ (not in Python and Java, as these do not have pointers). This is possible only because arrays are always continuous. So, the initial address can be referenced to a pointer and the rest can be used by relative accessing. Another way is to allocate a chunk of memory and assign it to a pointer, which is known as Dynamic Memory Allocation in C/C++. By using pointers, the limit on the number of elements or the size of an array can be removed. Arrays are defined in the form of lists. Even though Python doesn't have pointers, lists are, by default, designed in a dynamic way without any limit.

Some points to be noted about an array include:

- It is a continuous chunk of memory with equally sized blocks.
- The subscript always begins with 0 and goes till n–1, which is also continuous.

- Any memory location can be directly accessed using its subscript.
- Static arrays have issues like memory wastage and memory leak and has constraints over the size. These are overcome by using dynamic arrays, or Dynamic Memory Allocation (DMA), using pointers.
- Since it is a continuous chunk of memory, it has internal issues like fragmentation and memory leaks.
- This is the basic and naive data structure. Many other data structures are built using arrays.

Python lists have properties similar to an array, but don't require any size for declaration. They can continuously grow, with the elements being added into it, and are thus designed in a dynamic manner. Hence, lists overcome the problem of memory wastage and memory leak of arrays, as only the required memory blocks are associated with the list variable. Apart from these properties, Python lists have a special property. They can contain data of any types within the same lists, which is not possible in generic arrays in other programming languages. Thus, Python lists are better than basic array implementation in programming languages like C/C++. But a constraint for Python list is, as it is dynamic the elements may not be mandatorily stored in consecutive locations. Traditionally, however, arrays were designed for continuous memory locations only.

10.2.2 Lists Implementation

Python lists can be initialized in one of the following ways. The list can be created empty or with elements.

```
a = [] //empty list
a = [1,2,3,4,5] //list with 5 elements
a = [] * (5) //Empty list of size 5.
```

Once the list is created, elements can be accessed using the subscript. To assign a value '1' in the 4th position of the list created above, a[3] = 1 can be used. Such is the accessing of elements done using subscript. One additional property in lists is that lists can have data of any type unlike arrays.

10.2.3 The Operations

Once the list is declared by using either of the above ways, it is ready and settled in the memory. The basic operations on lists are:

- Insertion
- Deletion
- Merging

10.2.3.1 Insertion The only way to insert a new element into a list is to assign it to a specific subscript. So to insert, along with the element, the subscript is mandatory. For example, if '2' is to be inserted into 'a' at index 3, we have to initiate a[3] with '2', that is, 'a[3]=2'. Now '2' is inserted at subscript 3 of list 'a', but this may have multiple cases.

Case 1

Consider a[3] is empty, then inserting '2' will engage the location and '2' will then occupy the memory space 'a[3]' as shown in Figure 10.4.

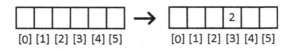

Figure 10.4   Inserting in an empty location.

Case 2

Consider a[3] is already occupied, then inserting '2' will overwrite the content in the location and '2' will occupy the memory space 'a[3]' as shown in Figure 10.5. Now, the old data in the location will be completely lost.

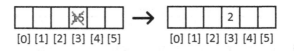

Figure 10.5   Inserting in an occupied location.

This is the only default available way for inserting elements into the array. To insert without the loss of existing data, the following algorithm is designed and implemented in Python.

Start from the penultimate element of the array, that is, index n-2. Move every element to the right by 1 position until the index where the new element is to be inserted is reached. Now, assign the location with the new value. All the elements before the index remain unchanged.

Python pseudocode 10.1: Insertion of an element

```
Loop i from lenght-1 to index
    Assign a[i] to a[i+1]
Assign the new element to a[index]
```

Another advantage of using Python lists is that functions like this are pre-defined and can be simply called for usage. This function is called as 'list.insert(index ,element)'.

10.2.3.2 Deletion The only way to delete an element is by using its subscript. So, to delete an element, its subscript is mandatory. If the subscript of an element is not known, then the element is searched in the list and then deleted. Deleting an element in the middle of the list will move all the following elements to the left, which is depicted in the following algorithm.

Start from the index next to the element to be deleted. Move every element to the left by one position until the end. Finally, free/delete the last element, as it will be duplicated. All the elements before the particular index remain unchanged, as shown in the pseudocode 10.2.

Python pseudocode 10.2: Deletion of an element

```
def delete(a[ ], element)
        index = 0
      Loop i in a
      if a[i]=element
            then,
              index = i
              break
    Loop i from index+1 to n-1
      Assign a[i] to a[i-1]
        Delete a[i-1]
        Return element
```

Just like insert, this function is also pre-defined in Python in the name of remove, called as 'list.remove(element)'.

10.2.3.3 Merging   Another notable operation on lists is merging two lists. This is basically concatenating the contents of the list into a new list. In addition, some patterns can be followed while merging the lists, as in all elements in odd indices of the merged list are from list1 and all elements in even indices are from list2. This operation is rarely used. In normal merge, it is creating a new list with list1 elements and appending list2 elements behind it. This utility is also predefined in Python as 'list1+list2'. This is achieved through operator overloading of the '+' operator. This is an instance to feel that lists are actually implemented as a class in Python.

10.2.3.4 Some More Operations   There are many other utility functions defined for lists. These can be used in basic read, write or modify functionalities of the list. Table 10.1 has a list of available predefined functions, a brief description and complexity of the same.

Other than these built-in functions, there are some operators overloaded for special utilities. All the available operators for list are shared in Table 10.2.

It is time to move to the next data structure, the stack!

Table 10.1   Pre-Defined Functions for Lists

FUNCTION	DESCRIPTION
List.append(element)	Appends the new element to the end of the list
List.count(element)	Returns the number of instances of the given element, if it is present in the list
List.extend(sequence)	Appends the elements of the sequence into the list
List.index(element)	Searches for the first instance of the element in the list and returns the index
List.pop( )	Removes and returns the last element from the list. This function can also take an optional argument, which is the index of the element to be removed and returned.
List.reverse( )	Reverses the given list
List.sort( )	Sorts the given list in ascending order. A comparison function may be given as an optional argument, based on which it will be sorted.

Table 10.2   Operators Available for Lists

OPERATOR	SYNTAX	DESCRIPTION
Length	Len(list)	Returns the length of the list
Concatenation	List1 + list2	Concatenates list1 and list2 and returns a new list.
Repetition	[element] * number	Creates a list with repeating the element for the specified number of times.
Membership	x in ['x', 'y', 'z']	Returns 'True' or 'False' signifying if the given element is present in the given list or not.
Iteration	for i in list: print i	Traverses through each element in the list.

10.3 Stack

A stack is a non-primitive data structure. It is a linear data structure designed only with linear access and not random access, with the data stored in continuous memory locations. Consider a pile of books as shown in Figure 10.6 or a stack of files. As the books lie one on top of the other, the data will be visualized as one above another. To take a book from the bottom, the books in the top must be removed and kept aside, so that the pile won't collapse. Once the required book is taken, the remaining books can be replaced above the pile. However, for ready access, only the book on the top of the pile will be available. The same is the case with the stack data structure, since to access an element we must traverse across the elements above it (in preceding memory locations). Always only the contents of the first cell will be readily available. The visual representation of a stack is shown in Figure 10.7.

Figure 10.6   Stack of books.

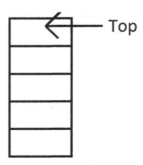
Top

Figure 10.7   Visual representation of a stack.

As shown in Figure 10.7, the first element of the stack is indicated by a 'TOP' pointer. This is the only way of accessing any element in the stack, thus forcing linear access. The movement of the data in the stack is commonly termed as Last In First Out (LIFO). An element that comes first into the stack is placed at the bottom, and all the new elements will be placed one above the other. So now, the element that came first always exists at the bottom of the stack. While removing the elements, the latest element will always move out first as it is present at the top of the stack. All the elements will be removed in the order of new to old and the element at the base of the stack will be last to be removed. This is termed as LIFO, as the last element comes out first.

Some points to be noted about a stack are:

- It stores elements in continuous memory locations.
- Only the top element of the stack can be accessed, using the TOP pointer.
- Accessing any other element is by linear traversal using the TOP pointer.
- The movement of data is LIFO, so in reading the data it will be in reverse of the order in which they were placed in the stack.

10.3.1 Working

As stacks are stored in continuous memory, it may face problems like memory constraints and fragmentation issues. So, it is implemented using lists in Python. There are only three notable operations over a stack. They are:

- Push
- Pop
- Top

10.3.1.1 Push

Push is the act of adding an element into the stack. It is given this name as we push the data into the top of the stack. Any data can be placed only on the top of the stack, so if you want the stack to be in a specific order, rearrange the elements in that order and push it one by one. It is known that stacks do not have any size restriction. So to push an element, no other parameter is required. Also it is important to update and maintain the TOP pointer, since losing the TOP pointer or misplacing it will cause loss of data. Loss of data means data is present in the memory, in an unknown location, merely as garbage.

Python pseudocode 10.3 for Push operation

```
Pseudocode for Push

1 Assign the new element to a[size]
2 Update Top pointer to a[size]
3 Size++
```

Initially, size will be 0, and TOP pointed to null.

As an example for better understanding, assume we push 2,3,1,4 into stack 'a', which is initially empty. Figure 10.8 illustrates pushing 2, 3, 1, 4 into stack 'a'.

10.3.1.2 Pop Pop is the operation of removing an element from the stack. In stack, we cannot decide which element is to be removed. Pop will always remove the data at the top of the stack. TOP pointer plays the role in pointing to the element at the top of the stack. If the TOP pointer is not consistently maintained, then pop may not work as expected. Similarly, after removing the top element, the TOP pointer should be updated to the next element, otherwise the entire stack will be lost. When the stack is empty, pop should not work. Else, it will result in a memory exception.

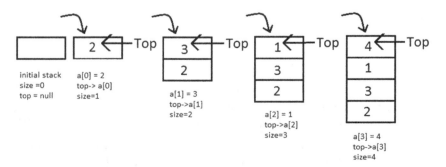

Figure 10.8   Illustration of pushing 2,3,1,4 into stack 'a'.

Python pseudocode 10.4 for Pop operation

Pseudocode for Pop is presented:

```
1 If stack is not empty
2 Then
3     Temp = value at Top
4     Stack[size - 1 ] = 0
5     Size--
6     Update Top to stack[size-1]
7     Return Temp
8 Else
9     Return 0 or any delimiter to show stack is empty
```

An instance to pop from stack 'a' containing 2,3,1,4. Figure 10.9 illustrates the pop operation.

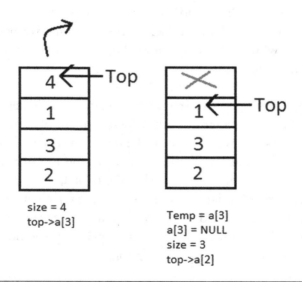

size = 4
top->a[3]

Temp = a[3]
a[3] = NULL
size = 3
top->a[2]

Figure 10.9 Pop operation illustration.

10.3.1.3 Top Top is the simplest operation in a stack. It just returns the element in the top of the stack and leaves the stack unchanged. Again, this should not work when the stack is empty, else it might produce some memory exceptions. It is solely dependent on the TOP pointer. If there has been any inconsistency in maintaining the TOP pointer at the time of Push or Pop, this function wouldn't have worked as expected. The top operation is also referred as the peek operation in some popular implementations.

Python pseudocode 10.5 for Top operation

Pseudocode for Top operation is presented below:

```
1 If stack is not empty
2   Then
3 Return value at Top
4   Else
5 Return 0 or any delimiter to show stack is empty
```

An instance to find Top from stack 'a' containing 2,3,1,4.

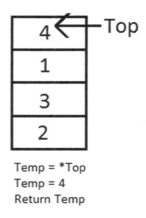

Figure **10.10**   Top operation and its result from a sample stack.

Figure 10.10 illustrates the Top operation.

A simple piece of code is presented below where the stack operation with Python has been carried out. One can observe that it is a very simple approach (Figure 10.11).

Once the code is executed, then one can get the results as presented in Figure 10.12.

It's time to move to the queue which is in the queue next.

```
list_one = [1,2,3,4,5,6,7,8]
print ("Initial Stack", list_one)

print ("Can we push an element on to the stack??")
list_one.append(9)
print ("Post Push (grown stack)", list_one)

print ("can we do a pop from the stack? Means, 9 out")
list_one.pop()
print ("Post POP (shrinked stack)", list_one)

print ("can we do a  peep? Returning the last value from the stack")
index_for_top = len (list_one) -1
print ("Length of the stack is", len(list_one))
print ("Post Peep (Top of the stack)", list_one [index_for_top])
```

Figure 10.11   Top operation and its result from a sample stack.

```
================= RESTART: F:/Python Playlist/Shriram/DS4.py ========
Initial Stack [1, 2, 3, 4, 5, 6, 7, 8]
Can we push an element on to the stack??
Post Push (grown stack) [1, 2, 3, 4, 5, 6, 7, 8, 9]
can we do a pop from the stack? Means, 9 out
Post POP (shrinked stack) [1, 2, 3, 4, 5, 6, 7, 8]
can we do a  peep? Returning the last value from the stack
Length of the stack is 8
Post Peep (Top of the stack) 8
>>>
```

Figure 10.12   Execution result for the code presented as Figure 10.11.

10.4 Queue

Queue is a non-primitive linear data structure. It is a linear data structure designed with linear access and restricting random access. This also stores data in continuous memory locations. Based on all these descriptions, it seems like the same as arrays and stacks. But this is not the case. It has its own uniqueness in organizing the data and accessing it. This is the most common data structure that can be seen in our day-to-day lives. It is designed after the queues that are used to organize people in crowded areas. In the queue of people shown in Figure 10.13; when a new person enters, he stands at the end of the queue. When the counter is open, the first person moves out. Then, the second person moves, and this continues. So, if a person standing in the middle of the queue wants to come out, then either all the people before him should come out or all the people behind him should come out. Once the person gets out, the others can return to the original position. Similarly, in this structure, the first data is always readily accessible. The visual representation of the queue is shown in Figure 10.13.

Figure 10.13   Queue of people in a counter.

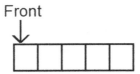

Figure 10.14   Visual representation of a queue.

As shown in Figure 10.14, the first element of the queue is indicated by the front pointer and can be accessed directly. Whereas, the rear end of the queue is maintained by the rear pointer. The movement of data across this structure is in the order of 'First In First Out (FIFO)'. An element that comes in first will go out first, as it is in straightforward motion only. Any new element that comes into the queue is placed after the rear pointer, and then the rear pointer is updated. A major difference between the stack and queue is that the elements are removed out in the same order as they enter in case of queues, whereas in stacks, the data is removed in the reverse order.

Some points to be noted about queues are:

- It stores elements in continuous memory locations.
- Only the first element of the queue can be accessed, using the 'FIRST' pointer.
- The end of the queue is marked by the 'REAR' pointer.

- Accessing the elements is possible only through linear traversal using the FIRST pointer.
- Movement of data is FIFO, so while reading the data it will be in same order in they came in.

There are three types of queues

- Single-ended Queue (The normal queue)
- Double-ended Queue (DEQue)
- Priority Queue

10.4.1 Single-ended Queue

Single-ended queues are one-way queues. The data can move only in a forward direction. The elements enter at the rear and leave from the front. Consider a boarding queue in the airport. The queue shown in Figure 10.15 is one such queue. Here, the passengers can enter into the queue, but not come back out. Once their procedure is over, they will move on to the next counter or lounge or aircraft. But they cannot come back out of the queue. Similar is the case with this data structure, elements can enter only at the rear end and can exit only at the front. (Readers can explore double-ended queues easily with this knowledge.)

Figure 10.15   One-way queue.

As shown in Figure 10.16, Enqueue is based on the Rear pointer and Dequeue is based on Front pointer. Only the Front pointer is accessible, whereas the Rear pointer is for internal reference.

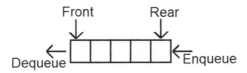

Figure 10.16 Visualization of single-ended queues.

10.4.2 Working

Queues also store the data in continuous memory locations. Thus, it is also implemented using list in Python. There are only three basic operations supported in the data structure. They are:

- Enqueue
- Dequeue
- Front

10.4.2.1 Enqueue This is the operation of adding an element into the queue. Any data can be added to the end of the queue. So, if you want the queue to have the data in some order, arrange the data in the same order and Enqueue it one by one into the queue. As the position cannot be determined by us, no other parameter is required for the function. It is always important to internally update the Rear pointer and maintain it correctly after every Enqueue operation. If the Rear pointer is not consistently maintained, data might be lost as any new data is added only based on this pointer. Inconsistency in the Rear pointer may result in two cases, overwriting of data – losing some old data or discontinuity within the queue that will collapse the whole structure.

Python pseudocode 10.6 for Enqueue operation

```
Pseudo code for enqueue:

1      If Queue is empty
2     Then,
3       Assign data in queue[0]
4       Front->queue[0]
5       Rear->queue[1]
6       Increment size
7     Else,
8       Assign data to Rear
9       Increment Rear
10      Increment size
```

Initially, size will be 0 and Front, Rear will be NULL.

Let's Enqueue 2,3,1,4 into a queue 'a', which is initially empty. The entire scenario is presented as Figure 10.17.

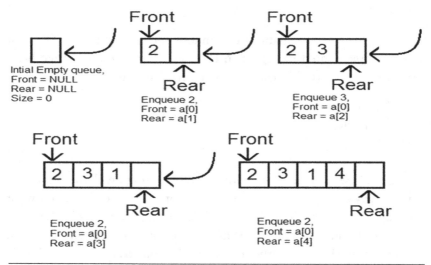

Figure 10.17   Illustration of Enqueue in an empty queue.

10.4.2.2 Dequeue   Dequeue is the complement for Enqueue. It is the process of removing the element out of the queue. As the queue is one way, the elements can come out only in the front. As said previously, the elements come out in the order they were sent in. The Front pointer marks the first element, and the process of Dequeue solely depends on it. So, after removing every element, it is equally important to consistently update the Front pointer. Failing to update the same would cause the loss of all the data. A queue with only a Rear pointer and no Front pointer is no use and the data will be treated as garbage only. The pseudocode for Dequeue is shared below. Another important point to notice is that when the queue is empty, access to the pointer will result in memory exceptions. Thus, a base case for checking the queue is not empty when added in the algorithm.

Python pseudocode 10.7 for Dequeue operation

```
Pseudocode for dequeue:
1  If Queue is not empty
2    Then,
3        Temp = value at Front
4        Increment Front
5  Decrement size
6  Return Temp
7    Else,
8        Return 0 or a delimiter to specify queue is empty
```

Can we Dequeue 2 times from a queue 'a' containing 2,3,1,4? Yes, one can refer to Figure 10.18 to understand the entire process.

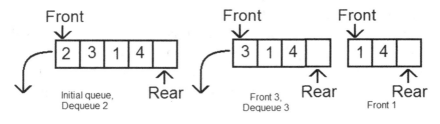

Figure 10.18   Dequeue illustration.

Solution

10.4.2.3 Front   This is similar to the function 'top' in stack. It is just reading what the first element in the data structure is, without disturbing it. Thus, it is the simplest operation of the data structure. This is fully based on the Front pointer, which is to be maintained properly by the Dequeue operation. Again, this should not work when the queue is empty, as it might result in memory exceptions.

Python pseudocode 10.8 for Front operation

```
Pseudocode for Front operation:
1  If Queue is not empty
2    Then,
3        Return value at front
4    Else,
5        Return 0 or a delimiter to specify queue is empty
```

Let's find the Front of a queue 'a' containing 3, 1, 4. (Figure 10.19)

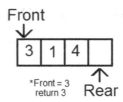

Figure 10.19   Front operation and result in a sample queue.

10.4.3 Priority Queue

A priority queue in a nutshell is a normal queue with a priority for each element. Consider the scenario in Figure 10.20, which is a function hall or theatre with seats. But the catch is the first row alone has royal seats, while the other rows have normal seats. The royal seats are for special or VIP visitors. The normal seats are for the normal people. Here all the people come in a queue, but the prioritized members will come to the front, and the normal person will go behind all other priority members. It is similar is the priority queue. A priority queue maintains priority for each element. It works as a queue with applied priority.

Figure 10.20   Priority seats in a theatre.

Basically, in priority queues, the data doesn't follow the FIFO order. The order of data coming out is according to the order of their priority. So, the data gets into the queue, gets reordered based on priority, and comes out. Generally, order of priority will be from lower to higher, i.e., element with priority value 0 will come first. This can be changed based on design.

A simple piece of code is presented below where some of the queue operations are presented and results follow (Figure 10.21, Figure 10.22).

```
list_one = [1,2,3,4,5,6,7,8]
print ("Initial Queue", list_one)

print ("Can we Insert an element on to the queue??")
list_one.append(9)
print ("Post Insert (grown queue)", list_one)

print ("can we do a delete from the Queue? From the front")
list_one.pop(0)
print ("Post POP (shrinked queue)", list_one)

print ("can we do a  peep? Returning the last value from the queue")
index_for_last_element = len (list_one) -1
print ("Length of the queue is", len(list_one))
print ("Post Peep (Last element of the queue)", list_one [index_for_last_element])

print ("can we print the first element of the queue?")
index = len (list_one)
index_for_first_element= len (list_one)-(index)
print ("The queue now", list_one)
print ("Post Peep (First element of the queue, Zeroth element technically)", list_one [index_for_first_element])
```

Figure 10.21   Queue with Python.

```
Python 3.7.3 (v3.7.3:ef4ec6ed12, Mar 25 2019, 21:26:53) [MSC v.1916 32 bit
1)] on win32
Type "help", "copyright", "credits" or "license()" for more information.
>>>
================= RESTART: F:/Python Playlist/Shriram/DS4.py ==============
Initial Queue [1, 2, 3, 4, 5, 6, 7, 8]
Can we Insert an element on to the queue??
Post Insert (grown queue) [1, 2, 3, 4, 5, 6, 7, 8, 9]
can we do a delete from the Queue? From the front
Post POP (shrinked queue) [2, 3, 4, 5, 6, 7, 8, 9]
can we do a  peep? Returning the last value from the queue
Length of the queue is 8
Post Peep (Last element of the queue) 9
can we print the first element of the queue?
The queue now [2, 3, 4, 5, 6, 7, 8, 9]
Post Peep (First element of the queue, Zeroth element technically) 2
>>> |
```

Figure 10.22   Results for the code presented as Figure 10.21.

A very important point must be reiterated here. Readers are prompted to try these learnings practically to have a better and stronger understanding.

Can we learn the next concept? Enumeration is the one.

10.5 Zip, Enumerate and Dictionaries

We all know Zip and we have been using it to compress files. Can we do zip with Python? Yes, but it is a bit different. We can zip two lists or Tuples together as one with a zip. An instance shall help us with easier understanding. A code is presented to perform zipping with Python as Figure 10.23. Results are presented subsequently as Figure 10.24.

```
List_One = [1,2,3,4,'a','b']
List_Two = ["Sachin", "Tendulkar"]
Tuple_One = (1,2,3,4,5,6,7)
print ("\n let's Zip everything together !!!" )
print (list(zip(List_One, List_Two, Tuple_One)))

List_One = [1,2,3,4,'a','b','c']
List_Two = ["Sachin", "Tendulkar","is","the","Greatest","of","all"]
Tuple_One = (1,2,3,4,5,6,7)
print ("\n let's Zip everything together !!!" )
print (list(zip(List_One, List_Two, Tuple_One)))

# Remember, it merges the lists and tuples together as a List!!
```

Figure 10.23   Code for zipping.

```
Python 3.7.3 (v3.7.3:ef4ec6ed12, Mar 25 2019, 21:26:53) [MSC v.1916 32 bit (Inte
l)] on win32
Type "help", "copyright", "credits" or "license()" for more information.
>>>
================= RESTART: F:/Python Playlist/Shriram/DS5.py =================

 let's Zip everything together !!!
[(1, 'Sachin', 1), (2, 'Tendulkar', 2)]

 let's Zip everything together !!!
[(1, 'Sachin', 1), (2, 'Tendulkar', 2), (3, 'is', 3), (4, 'the', 4), ('a', 'Grea
test', 5), ('b', 'of', 6), ('c', 'all', 7)]
>>>
```

Figure 10.24   Results for the code presented as Figure 10.23.

It is now the time to learn Enumerate (Figure 10.25). Enumerate helps to keep track of the iterations. (At times you must do this.) It is a kind of automatic counter it provides.

```
# Can we Learn Enumerate?
# It is Simple and Effective.
some_list = [1,2,3,4,5,6,7,8,9,10]
for counter, value in enumerate(some_list):
    print(counter, value)
# Here, you shall get the index position, with ease
Python 3.7.3 (v3.7.3:ef4ec6ed12, Mar 25 2019, 21:26:53) [MSC v.1916 32 bit (:
1)] on win32
Type "help", "copyright", "credits" or "license()" for more information.
>>>
================= RESTART: F:/Python Playlist/Shriram/DS6.py ==============:
0 1
1 2
2 3
3 4
4 5
5 6
6 7
7 8
8 9
9 10
>>> |
```

Figure 10.25   Enumerate example.

Let's learn about dictionaries in Python.

A dictionary is a built-in data structure that is used to store a collection of key-value pairs. It is also known as an associative array or a hash map in other programming languages. Dictionaries are extremely useful for quickly looking up values based on their associated keys. A simple example is presented as Figure 10.26 where one can see how the dictionary is created with Python. Results are presented in the same figure which shall be handy for the reader to visualize the dictionary usage.

```
File Edit Format Run Options Window ⊦
# Dictionary Example
my_dictionary = {
    "brand": "HP",
    "model": "Laptop",
    "year": 2019
}
print(my_dictionary)
```

```
File Edit Shell Debug Options Window Help
Python 3.7.3 (v3.7.3:ef4ec6ed12, Mar 25 2019, 21:26:53) [MSC v.1916 32 bit (Inte
l)] on win32
Type "help", "copyright", "credits" or "license()" for more information.
>>>
============= RESTART: F:/Python Playlist/Shriram/Dictionary.py =============
{'brand': 'HP', 'model': 'Laptop', 'year': 2019}
>>> |
```

Figure 10.26 Dictionary in Python.

Can someone access the dictionary? Yes, it is possible, and an instance is presented below as Figure 10.27 followed by results being presented as Figure 10.28.

```
# Here you go! This is how we create dictionary.
# Key / Value pair
# Dictionary Example
my_dictionary = {
    "brand": "HP",
    "model": "Laptop",
    "year": 2019
}
print(my_dictionary)

# Here you go, this is how we can access the dictionary.
x = my_dictionary["model"]
print (x)

x = my_dictionary["year"]
print (x)

# Here you go, we can change the value for an element.
my_dictionary["year"] = 1983
my_dictionary["model"] = "DeskTop"
print(my_dictionary)

# To check if a particular key is present in the dictionary.
if "model" in my_dictionary:
    print("Yes, 'model' is one of the keys in the thisdict dictionary")

# Can we find length of a Dictionary
print(len(my_dictionary))
```

Figure 10.27 Dictionary access in Python.

```
Python 3.7.3 (v3.7.3:ef4ec6ed12, Mar 25 2019, 21:26:53) [MSC v.1916 32 bit (Inte
l)] on win32
Type "help", "copyright", "credits" or "license()" for more information.
>>>
============= RESTART: F:\Python Playlist\Shriram\Dictionary.py =============
{'brand': 'HP', 'model': 'Laptop', 'year': 2019}
Laptop
2019
{'brand': 'HP', 'model': 'DeskTop', 'year': 1983}
Yes, 'model' is one of the keys in the thisdict dictionary
3
>>> |
```

Figure 10.28 The dictionary access.

One can delete a dictionary with ease. As shown in Figure 10.29, one can use del <dictionary_name> to delete the dictionary.

```
my_dictionary = {
  "brand": "HP",
  "model": "Laptop",
  "year": 2019
}
print(my_dictionary)
print ("Can we delete the entire dictionary? \n")

del my_dictionary
```

Figure 10.29 Deletion of a dictionary.

Well, this chapter could have been a little intense. But, this is a very important chapter for the learners.

Readers can watch the following YouTube lectures to gain more understanding:

Python – Directory operations in Python – https://youtu.be/SmjpZV-6BCY

Python – Data structures – Lists in Python – https://youtu.be/4bIqKeuyhu0

Data structures – Stack in Python (Push, Pop, Peep) – https://youtu.be/vmOmv_QApb0

Queue implementation in Python – Easy method – https://youtu.be/ke3U2kqVDa8

Data structures – Dictionary, zip and enumerate in Python – https://youtu.be/SlmuP8BsXuM

Key Points to Remember

- A data structure is a format for storing the data in an organized manner.
- Data structure is all about learning how to store and retrieve data in an effective and efficient manner.
- The simplest data structure is an array.
- Data structures can be classified as primitive and non-primitive data structures.
- Arrays – Basic linear data structure which stores elements of the same type in continuous memory locations.
- Python lists – List is a class in Python which is implemented as a data structure to store a collection of elements of various types in a sequential pattern in continuous/non-continuous memory locations.
- Insertion into a list – The operation of adding a new element into a list.
- Deletion from a list – The operation of removing an element.
- Queues are non-primitive linear data structures that follow the FIFO movement of data.
- Queues allow insertion in the REAR pointer and removal in a pointer.
- There are three types of queues – single-ended queue (one-way motion), double-ended queue (two-way motion) and priority queue (multi-level queue).
- We can zip two lists or tuples together as one with a zip.
- A dictionary is a built-in data structure that is used to store a collection of key-value pairs.

Further Reading

For further learning one can refer to:

Python official website – https://www.python.org/
Awesome Python – https://github.com/vinta/awesome-python

11

CLASSES AND OBJECTS

LEARNING OBJECTIVES

After reading this chapter, readers will have learned:

- How to create classes
- What an object is
- Class method and self
- init – a constructive approach
- Destructor – Let's destroy
- Access specifiers
- Some key points to remember.

11.1 Introduction

A class in Python is an example or template used to create objects, or instances of them. It outlines the characteristics (data) and operations (functions) that the class's objects will possess. Classes offer a mechanism to arrange and structure code into reusable, self-contained units and are essential to object-oriented programming (OOP).

This section shall detail the classes and objects in Python. Remember, Python is object-oriented.

11.2 Classes and Objects in Python

Readers might have learnt the classes and objects with C++ or Java earlier. It is time that we learn that in Python. How do we define a class in Python?

DOI: 10.1201/9781032712673-11

class <class_name>:

     ....

     ....

     ....

That's it! You created a class.

What is an object is the next question to be answered. It is an instance of a class. Many objects together form a class. A simple code is presented below as Figure 11.1, where class and object are both presented. One can see that dot (.) is used to access the class like it is in C++.

```
# this is an example for the class and object!
class my_class:                        # This is the class name
    member_variable= 12                # This is the member variable
my_object=my_class()                   # Here, we create an object. (Instantiate)
print (my_object.member_variable)      # Accessing the variable through the object
my_object.member_variable = 15         # Assigning a new value to the variable.
print (my_object.member_variable)      # Printing it.
```

```
Python 3.7.3 (v3.7.3:ef4ec6ed12, Mar 25 2019, 21:26:53) [MSC v.1916 32 bit (Inte
l)] on win32
Type "help", "copyright", "credits" or "license()" for more information.
>>>
=============== RESTART: F:/Python Playlist/Shriram/class1.py ===============
12
15
>>>
```

Figure 11.1   Class and object in Python.

It is important to know the class method and self in Python. It might look little difficult to understand in the first shot. But it is easy.

In Python, self is a conventional name used for the first parameter in a method of a class. It represents the instance of the class and allows you to access the attributes and methods of that instance within the class. While self is a conventional name, you can technically name the first parameter of a method anything you like, but using self is a widely accepted and recommended practice.

A typical example is presented below as Figure 11.2, where self is used. One more example is presented as Figure 11.3 where the conventional naming practice as self is changed and the result is also presented.

```
class my_class:                           # This is called class
    my_variable= 10                       # It is class variable.
    def my_function (self):               # This is called the class method (See self inside)
        print ("Here you go, this is called class method .... \n")
my_obj=my_class()                         # Creatng an object
print (my_obj.my_variable)                # Accessing the variable through the object
my_obj.my_function()                      # calling the function.
```

```
Python 3.7.3 (v3.7.3:ef4ec6ed12, Mar 25 2019, 21:26:53) [MSC v.1916 32 bit (Intel)] on win32
Type "help", "copyright", "credits" or "license()" for more information.
>>>
============== RESTART: F:/Python Playlist/Shriram/class2.py ==============
10
Here you go, this is called class method ....
```

Figure 11.2 'self' in Python.

```
class my_class:                           # This is called class
    my_variable= 10                       # It is class variable.
    def my_function (self):               # This is called the class method (See self inside)
        print ("Here you go, this is called class method .... \n")
my_obj=my_class()                         # Creatng an object
print (my_obj.my_variable)                # Accessing the variable through the object
my_obj.my_function()                      # calling the function.

class my_class1 ():                       # This is called class, this is also class!!!
    my_variable= 10                       # It is class variable.
    def my_function (myself):             # This is called the class method (See MYSELF inside)
        print ("Here you go, this is called class method .... \n")
my_obj=my_class()                         # Creatng an object
print (my_obj.my_variable)                # Accessing the variable through the object
my_obj.my_function()                      # calling the function.
```

```
============== RESTART: F:/Python Playlist/Shriram/class2.py ==============
10
Here you go, this is called class method ....


10
Here you go, this is called class method ....
```

Figure 11.3 'self' or 'myself' in Python.

11.3 __init__ and __del__

Readers might be aware of what a constructor is. If not, think of it in terms of cleaning the plate before taking food to consume. That is, we should initialize. A constructor is a method of initializing the object when it is created! Means, it gets called automatically.

In Python, __init__ (with double underscores on both sides) is a special method, often referred to as a constructor, that is used to initialize objects created from a class. It is automatically called when you create a new instance (object) of a class. The __init__ method allows you to set initial values for the object's attributes.

An example code is presented below as Figure 11.4 where readers can refer to the way in which it can be done.

```
class my_class :
    def __init__(self,value_init):   # See, first it is self, second is the argument
        print ("\n I am inside the class method")
        self.value_init=value_init
        print ("\n The Value is", value_init)
my_obj=my_class (16)
```

```
Python 3.7.3 (v3.7.3:ef4ec6ed12, Mar 25 2019, 21:26:53) [MSC v.1916 32 bit (In
l)] on win32
Type "help", "copyright", "credits" or "license()" for more information.
>>>
=============== RESTART: F:/Python Playlist/Shriram/class3.py ===============

I am inside the class method

The Value is 16
>>>
```

Figure 11.4 '__init__' usage.

Having discussed the constructor, it is only fair that we also discuss the destructor.

Destructor is just like washing the plate after eating food so that someone else can use it. It is opposite to the constructor, meaning that whatever is allocated is wiped off completely. To accomplish this, Python has __del__ and once the work is complete, this can be called.

It's less commonly used than __init and is typically not needed in most Python programs. It's important to note that the use of the __del__ method is often discouraged because it can lead to unpredictable behavior in some cases. The garbage collection process in Python is managed automatically.

An example is presented as Figure 11.5 for readers' easier understanding where __del__ is called. Once the deletion happens, the object cannot be accessed again.

```
class my_class :
    def _init_(self,value_init):  # See, first it is self, second is the argument
        print ("\n I am inside the class method")
        value=value_init
        print ("\n The Value is", value)
my_obj=my_class(16)
print (my_obj)

print ("\n Can we delete / destruct \n")
print (my_obj)
del my_obj
print (my_obj)
```

```
Python 3.7.3 (v3.7.3:ef4ec6ed12, Mar 25 2019, 21:26:53) [MSC v.1916 32 bit (Intel)] on win32
Type "help", "copyright", "credits" or "license()" for more information.
>>>
=============== RESTART: F:\Python Playlist\Shriram\class3.py ===============

I am inside the class method

The Value is 16

Can we delete / destruct

<_main_.my_class object at 0x037FA370>
Traceback (most recent call last):
  File "F:\Python Playlist\Shriram\class3.py", line 10, in <module>
    print (my_obj)
NameError: name 'my_obj' is not defined
```

Figure 11.5   '__del__' with Python.

11.4 Access Specifiers with Python

Access specifiers are not rigidly enforced in Python as they are in certain other programming languages, such as Java or C++. Python operates under the tenet that "we are all consenting adults here," implying that it can be trusted to adhere to naming standards and rules around method and attribute access. Though they are more akin to conventions than rigorous access specifiers, Python does offer certain tools to manage access to properties and functions.

Public can be accessed from anywhere. One should remember that, with the public way,

- It is free to access within the class, outside the class.
- . (dot) operator shall be used.

Private can be accessed only from within the class. This is safe.

- With (double underscore, access can be made)

A simple code presented below can be referred to understand the usage (Figure 11.6). One can observe the restrictions through a careful walkthrough of the same.

```
class my_class ():
    def __init__(self,value1, value2):
        self.variable1=value1          # Public
        self.__variable2=value2        # Private (__ makes it private)
    def show (self):
        print ("\n Can we access from class method, Value1", self.variable1)    #public.
        print ("\n Can we access from class method, Value2", self.__variable2) #Here, it is private.
my_obj=my_class(20,40)
my_obj.show()
print ("\n Can we access from main", my_obj.variable1)          # This is sucessful.
print ("\n Can we access from main, Value2", my_obj.__variable2) # This is failure.
```

```
Python 3.7.3 (v3.7.3:ef4ec6ed12, Mar 25 2019, 21:26:53) [MSC v.1916 32 bit (Intel)] on win32
Type "help", "copyright", "credits" or "license()" for more information.
>>>
=============== RESTART: F:/Python Playlist/Shriram/class4.py ===============

Can we access from class method, Value1 20

Can we access from class method, Value2 40

Can we access from main 20
Traceback (most recent call last):
  File "F:/Python Playlist/Shriram/class4.py", line 11, in <module>
    print ("\n Can we access from main, Value2", my_obj.__variable2) # This is failure.
AttributeError: 'my_class' object has no attribute '__variable2'
>>>
```

Figure 11.6 Access specifiers in Python.

One can also walk through below the videos to understand things better.

Classes and objects in Python, __init__ in Python – https://youtu.be/HLj548WHRxU

Destructors and access specifiers in Python – https://youtu.be/XWGwudG1rjE

Key Points to Remember

- A class in Python is an example or template used to create objects, or instances of them. It outlines the characteristics (data) and operations (functions) that the class's objects will possess.
- __init__ (with double underscores on both sides) is a special method, often referred to as a constructor, that is used to initialize objects created from a class.
- It's important to note that the use of the __del__ method is often discouraged because it can lead to unpredictable behavior in some cases.
- The garbage collection process in Python is managed automatically.
- Access specifiers are not rigidly enforced in Python as they are in certain other programming languages, such as Java or C++.

Further Reading

For further learning one can refer to:

Python official website – https://www.python.org/

Awesome Python – https://github.com/vinta/awesome-python

12

FUN LEARNING

LEARNING OBJECTIVES

After reading this chapter, readers will have learned:

- How to access CSV from Python
- NumPy
- SciPy
- NumPy vs. SciPy
- Intel distribution for Python
- Some key points to remember.

12.1 Introduction

Readers have come a long way in the learning process, and this is almost the last part of the book. It is fair that the readers are presented with some easy-to-learn content in this chapter. It will be fun and interesting too.

12.2 Accessing CSV from Python

CSV stands for Comma-Separated Values, and it is a simple and widely used file format for storing tabular data. In a CSV file, data is organized as a series of rows, with each row containing one or more fields separated by commas (or other delimiters such as semicolons or tabs). One can access this CSV files easily with Python and this section of the chapter deals with the same.

We have created a simple CSV file which has the content as revealed in Figure 12.1. One can use Microsoft Excel to create the CSV files through the save as option.

DOI: 10.1201/9781032712673-12

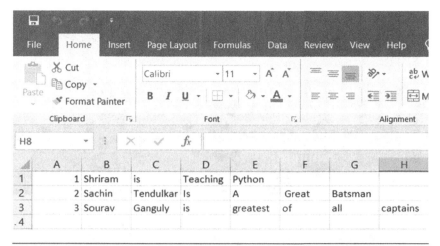

Figure 12.1 CSV file content.

The code and results on executing the code are presented as Figure 12.2. Importing the CSV module and using the methods appropriately will get the job done for us.

1_csv.py - C:/Users/Shriram K V/Desktop/Python/1_csv.py (3.7.4)

File   Edit   Format   Run   Options   Window   Help

```
import csv
with open('mydata.csv', 'r') as csvFile:
    csvcontent = csv.reader(csvFile)
    for r in csvcontent:
        print(r)
csvFile.close()
```

Python 3.7.4 Shell   —   □   ×

File Edit Shell Debug Options Window Help

```
Python 3.7.4 (tags/v3.7.4:e09359112e, Jul  8 2019, 20:34:20) [MSC v.1916 64 bit (AMD64)] on win3
2
Type "help", "copyright", "credits" or "license()" for more information.
>>>
============ RESTART: C:/Users/Shriram K V/Desktop/Python/1_csv.py ============
['1', 'Shriram', 'is ', 'Teaching', 'Python', '', '', '']
['2', 'Sachin ', 'Tendulkar', 'Is ', 'A ', ' Great ', 'Batsman', '']
['3', 'Sourav', 'Ganguly ', 'is ', 'greatest', 'of ', 'all ', 'captains']
>>>
```

Figure 12.2 CSV file access through Python.

One can read the CSV file into the dictionary as well with the below piece of code (Figure 12.3).

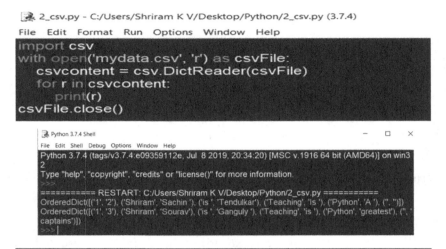

Figure 12.3 Reading the CSV file into a dictionary.

One can write into a CSV file easily with Python. One can have a look below at the piece of code where the methods are used to write content into the CSV file (Figure 12.4).

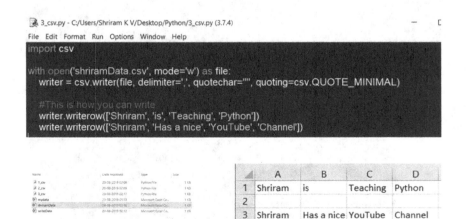

Figure 12.4 Writing content into the CSV.

12.3 NumPy

"Numerical Python," or NumPy, is the name of a popular open-source Python library for mathematical and numerical operations. Large, multi-dimensional arrays and matrices are supported, and a broad variety of sophisticated mathematical operations can be performed on these arrays. Often used in conjunction with other libraries for scientific computing and data analysis, including SciPy, pandas and Matplotlib, NumPy is a core library for data manipulation and analysis within the Python ecosystem.

NumPy's salient attributes and functionalities comprise:

- Multidimensional arrays: The main data structure in NumPy is the ndarray, or n-dimensional array. This data structure is useful for jobs that involve vectors, matrices and tensors since it allows you to work with arrays of different dimensions.
- NumPy offers an extensive collection of mathematical functions that can be used to carry out operations on arrays, such as additions, subtraction, multiplications and divisions, element-wise. Statistical procedures, linear algebra and other things are also supported.
- Broadcasting: NumPy makes broadcasting possible, which frequently eliminates the need for explicit loops and permits actions across arrays of various sizes and shapes to be carried out in a logical manner.
- Integration with C and Fortran: NumPy provides interfaces to C and Fortran libraries, enabling the integration of low-level Python code with these languages to boost efficiency.
- NumPy has functions for creating random distributions of data and random numbers, both of which are helpful in statistical analysis and simulations.
- Interoperability: NumPy may be easily combined with other libraries for data analysis, including Matplotlib for data presentation and pandas for data processing.

Because of its rapidity, the extensive ecosystem of dependent libraries and effective array handling, NumPy is a vital tool for Python activities related to scientific computing, Machine Learning and data analysis. It is an invaluable tool for scientists, engineers and data analysts working with numerical data in Python since it makes complex mathematical operations and data processing simpler.

How can someone install NumPy? (Figure 12.5)

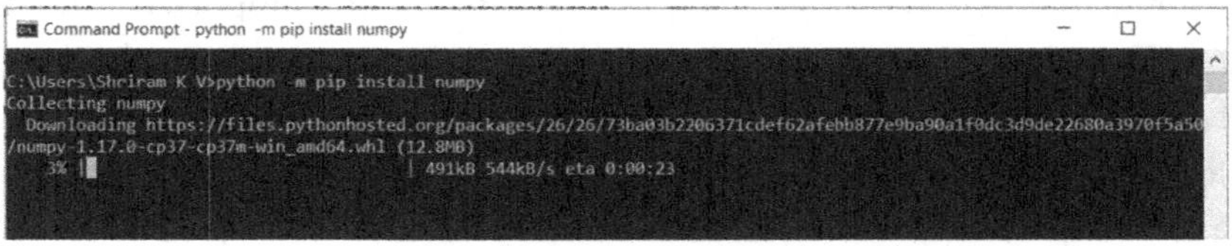

Figure 12.5 NumPy installation.

The command for the installation of NumPy is: python –m pip install numpy

Can we create an array first? We can create an array with Python lists using an array function. The type of array shall be determined automatically based on the content. a.dtype shall present the type of the data (Figure 12.6).

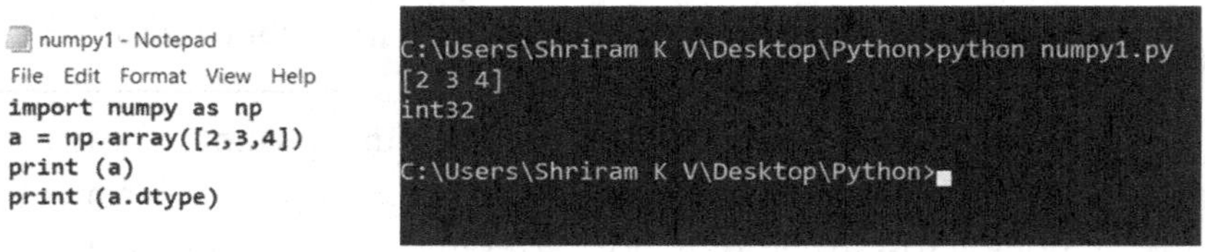

Figure 12.6 Array with NumPy.

One more example is presented as Figure 12.7.

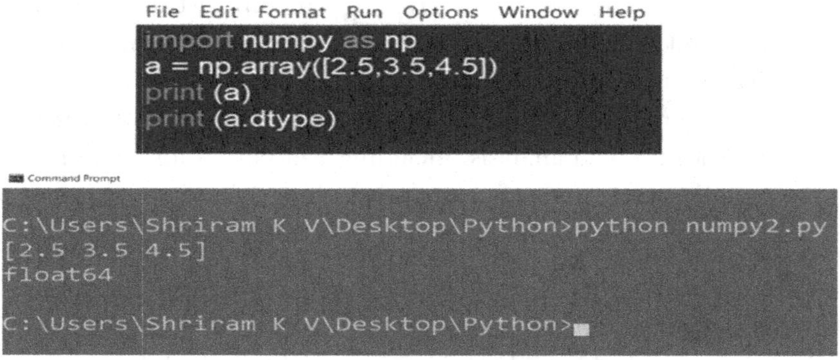

Figure 12.7 Array with NumPy.

NumPy transforms sequences of sequences into a two-dimensional array and one example is presented as Figure 12.8.

```
File   Edit   Format   Run   Options   Window   Help
import numpy as np
b = np.array([(1,2,3), (4,5,6), (7,8,9)])
print (b)
```

```
C:\Users\Shriram K V\Desktop\Python>python numpy3.py
[[1 2 3]
 [4 5 6]
 [7 8 9]]

C:\Users\Shriram K V\Desktop\Python>
```

Figure 12.8 NumPy – transformation to a two-dimensional array.

Zeros is a function supported by NumPy. This shall act as a place holder and is very useful. An example shall be handy and is presented in Figure 12.9.

```
File   Edit   Format   Run   Options   Window   Help
# Filling 0s and 1s are handy too!!
import numpy as np
b=np.zeros( (3,4) )
print (b)
c=np.ones( (3,4) )
print (c)
```

```
=========== RESTART: C:/Users/Shriram
[[0. 0. 0. 0.]
 [0. 0. 0. 0.]
 [0. 0. 0. 0.]]
[[1. 1. 1. 1.]
 [1. 1. 1. 1.]
 [1. 1. 1. 1.]]
>>>
```

Figure 12.9 Zeros with NumPy.

One more example shall be very handy here. We have also used np.arrange along with np.zeros and np.ones (Figure 12.10).

With NumPy one can find the min, max and sum so easily on the go. One can refer to the code presented below as Figure 12.11 to understand the usage.

```
File  Edit  Format  Run  Options  Window  Help
# Filling 0s and 1s are handy tool!
import numpy as np
b=np.zeros( (3,4) )  # To fill with zeros
print (b)
c=np.ones( (3,4) )  # To fill with ones
print (c)
d=np.arange( 10, 50, 2 ) #create sequences of numbers,
print (d)
```

```
=========== RESTART: C:\Users\Shriram K V\Desktop\Python\numpy5.py ===========
[[0. 0. 0. 0.]
 [0. 0. 0. 0.]
 [0. 0. 0. 0.]]
[[1. 1. 1. 1.]
 [1. 1. 1. 1.]
 [1. 1. 1. 1.]]
[10 12 14 16 18 20 22 24 26 28 30 32 34 36 38 40 42 44 46 48]
```

Figure 12.10   'np.arrange' method.

```
File  Edit  Format  Run  Options  Window  Help
import numpy as np
# We are going to find the sum, min and max.
a= np.array([1,2,3])
print(a.min())
print(a.max())
print(a.sum())
```

```
File  Edit  Shell  Debug  Options  Window  Help
Python 3.7.4 (tags/v3.7.4:e09359112e, Jul 8 2019, 20:34:20) [MSC v.1916 64 bit (AMD64
2
Type "help", "copyright", "credits" or "license()" for more information.
>>>
=========== RESTART: C:/Users/Shriram K V/Desktop/Python/numpy7.py =========
1
3
6
>>>
```

Figure 12.11   'min', 'max' and 'sum' with NumPy.

Can we learn SciPy? It is also very important and easy to learn.

12.4 SciPy

A vital part of the Python scientific computing ecosystem is SciPy, together with NumPy. It plays a critical role in domains like physics, biology, engineering, economics and data science and makes difficult mathematical and scientific computations easy for scientists, engineers and researchers to accomplish. Combining NumPy and SciPy offers a flexible and strong toolkit for utilizing Python to tackle a variety of scientific and technical problems.

One can install SciPy with pip install scipy command.

An open-source Python library called SciPy expands on NumPy's features and offers more functionality for a variety of technical and scientific computing applications. It frequently works in tandem with NumPy and other libraries to form a potent ecosystem for engineering and scientific applications. SciPy is quite helpful for tasks like signal and image processing, linear algebra, interpolation, optimization, integration, statistics, and more.

Among SciPy's main attributes and functionalities are:

- Optimization: For the solution of both linear and nonlinear optimization problems, SciPy provides a range of optimization techniques. This helps with model training in domains like Machine Learning and in scientific research to identify the best answers to challenging issues.
- Numerical integration functions, such as single and multiple definite integrals, are available in SciPy. This is useful for figuring out calculus, physics and engineering difficulties.
- SciPy offers a variety of interpolation methods that are helpful for estimating functions from discrete data points.
- Signal and image processing: Filtering, spectral analysis, and other signal processing activities are included in the package. It is appropriate for computer vision and image analysis because it also provides tools for working with images.
- Linear algebra: SciPy adds functionality to NumPy's linear algebra capabilities, allowing for the computation of eigenvalues and eigenvectors, the solution of linear equations, and a variety of matrix operations.
- Statistical functions: SciPy has an extensive collection of statistical functions for probability distributions, hypothesis testing, descriptive statistics and other applications. It's an important tool for testing hypotheses and performing statistical analysis.

- Special functions: The library has several special mathematical functions that are frequently utilized in a variety of scientific and engineering applications, including gamma functions and Bessel functions.
- Sparse matrices: Working with high-dimensional data and solving complex linear systems require the effective handling of sparse matrices, which SciPy provides.

12.5 NumPy and SciPy Differences

Although they are closely linked, NumPy and SciPy are two crucial libraries in the Python scientific computing ecosystem that have slightly different uses. The following are the main distinctions between SciPy and NumPy:

- NumPy is primarily concerned with supporting fundamental array operations and multidimensional arrays (ndarrays). With features for effective data manipulation and storage, it serves as the basis for Python's numerical operations.
- Building upon NumPy, SciPy offers a broad range of high-level functions and tools for a variety of scientific and technical computer applications. It has modules for linear algebra, statistics, signal processing, integration, interpolation, optimization and more.
- NumPy mostly offers mathematical operations, array manipulation and elementary linear algebra functionalities.
- SciPy is an extension of NumPy that provides sophisticated numerical methods and algorithms for handling intricate mathematical and scientific problems, including statistical analysis, interpolation, optimization and integration.
- NumPy concentrates on arrays and fundamental functions. Basic mathematical functions and ndarray manipulation functions are included.
- SciPy consists of multiple sub-packages, like SciPy, each devoted to a particular scientific or technical field. scipy.interpolate for interpolation, scipy.integrate for integration, optimize for optimization, and many more.

- NumPy is useful for basic mathematical computations and data preprocessing because it can perform basic data manipulation and numerical operations.
- SciPy is designed for use in scientific and technical applications. It may be used for tasks like signal processing, differential equation solution, numerical optimization and sophisticated statistical analysis.
- Since SciPy is based on NumPy, NumPy is automatically installed as a dependent when SciPy is installed.
- To utilize SciPy, you must first install NumPy as a requirement.

Having learnt the NumPy and SciPy, it is time to understand the distributions of Python. The most famous distribution for Python is Intel distribution.

12.6 The Intel Distribution for Python

The Intel distribution for Python improves the speed of common libraries and algorithms, especially data analytics, to yield better performance. The new optimization provides significant speedups for scikit-learn (a free software machine learning library), especially in NumPy (short for Numerical Python) and SciPy (Scientific Python) packages which are meant for performing various operations with the data. It also leverages Intel Data Analytics Acceleration Library (Intel DAAL). The performance speed can be seen to accelerate to around a whopping 140 times for several scikit-learn algorithms. Intel DAAL is a software development library that is highly optimized for Intel architecture processors and provides building blocks for all data analytics stages, from data preparation to data mining and Machine Learning.

The Intel distribution for Python includes accelerated packages for NumPy, SciPy and SKLEARN that are drop-in compatible with other similar community packages. Since these accelerated packages best utilize the Intel hardware already available, no code changes are needed.

The readers can visit https://intel.ly/33OWf5N to download the Intel distribution for Python.

As a first step to install and use the Intel distribution for Python, one has the option to go ahead with Intel AI Analytics Toolkit or Via Anaconda.

We shall choose the option of Anaconda and then the following steps are to be taken, one after another.

As shown in Figure 12.12, one must click the Anaconda prompt.

Next, one should update conda with the command "conda update conda". One would get the status completion message on correct execution (Figure 12.13).

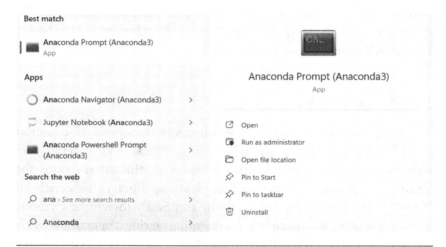

Figure 12.12   Anaconda prompt.

Figure 12.13   'conda' update.

Add Intel channel as the next step. Tell conda to choose Intel packages over default packages, when available. One should issue the command conda config --add channels intel (Figure 12.14).

```
(base) PS C:\Users\ShriramKV> conda config --add channels intel
```

Figure 12.14   Add intel channel.

As the next step, install Intel Distribution for Python* via conda. It is recommended that you create a new environment while installing. To install the core python3 environment, issue the command conda create -n idp intelpython3_core python=3.x. One can refer to the screenshot to understand the process (Figure 12.15).

```
(base) PS C:\Users\ShriramKV> conda create -n idp intelpython3_core python=3.9
WARNING: A conda environment already exists at 'C:\Users\ShriramKV\anaconda3\envs\idp'
Remove existing environment (y/[n])? y

Collecting package metadata (current_repodata.json): done
Solving environment: done
```

Figure 12.15   Installation of Intel Python.

Please note that "x" in "python=3.x" should signify which version of Python* you would like to install

Finally, activate the Conda environment (Figure 12.16).

■ Anaconda Powershell Prompt (anaconda3)

```
(base) PS C:\Users\ShriramKV> conda activate idp
(idp) PS C:\Users\ShriramKV>
```

Figure 12.16   Activate conda.

How can we validate if the installation has gone well? Simple. One should refer to Figure 12.17 to know how to do this.

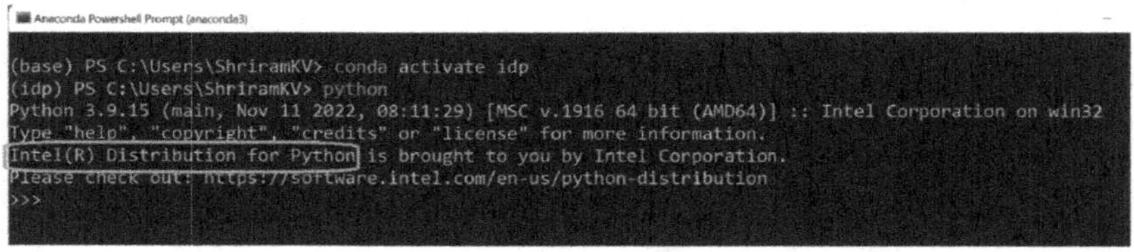

Figure 12.17 Validation.

Below is the piece of sample code (Figure 12.18) taken into consideration to run with the stock version Python and Intel Distribution for Python. One executed, one could note the time needed for the execution with both the variants of the Python (Figure 12.19).

```python
import numpy as np
import time

start = time.time()

rd = np.random.RandomState(88)
a = rd.randint(1,1000,(1000,1000))
y = rd.randint(1,1000,(1000))
res = np.linalg.solve(a,y)

end = time.time()

print(res)
print('Time Consuming:',end-start)
```

Figure 12.18 The sample code.

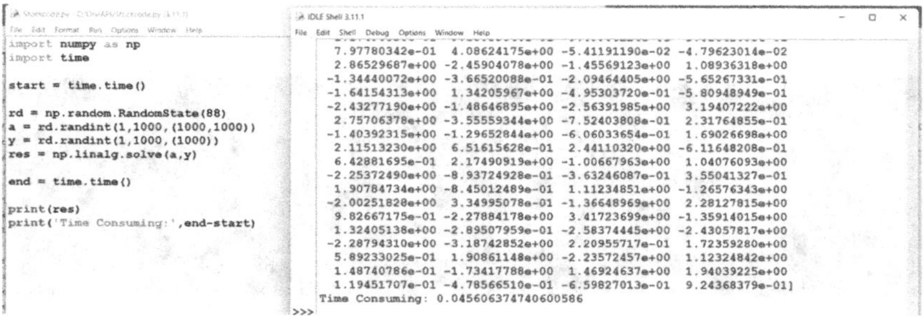

Figure 12.19 Time consumed with the stock version of Python.

To understand the difference the Intel distribution brings on the table, the same piece of code has been executed with the Intel Distribution for Python. One could see that there is a good difference in the performance and Intel Distribution has outperformed the stock version (Figure 12.20).

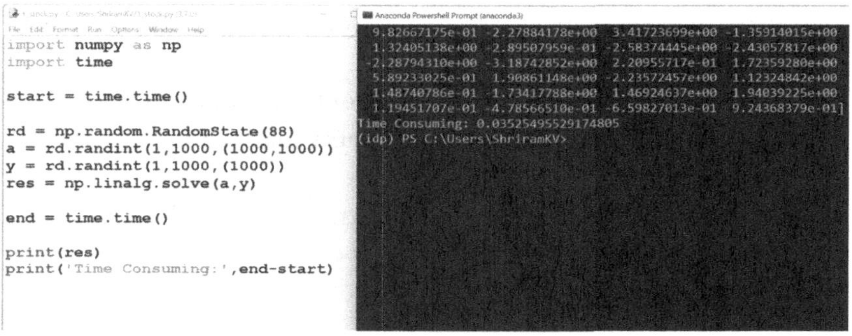

Figure 12.20 Time consumed with the Intel Python.

Readers can watch the following YouTube lectures to gain more understanding:

How to Access CSV files from Python? (Read, Write CSV) - https://youtu.be/S5viJ5sBj44

NumPy in Python - https://youtu.be/a8h7Eq-m9YA

Key Points to Remember

- CSV stands for Comma-Separated Values, and it is a simple and widely used file format for storing tabular data. In a CSV file, data is organized as a series of rows, with each row containing one or more fields separated by commas.
- SciPy expands on NumPy's features and offers more functionality for a variety of technical and scientific computing applications.
- For tasks like signal and image processing, linear algebra, interpolation, optimization, integration, statistics and more, SciPy is quite helpful.

- "Numerical Python," or NumPy, is the name of a well-liked open-source Python library for mathematical and numerical operations.
- SciPy is based on NumPy, NumPy is automatically installed as a dependent when SciPy is installed.
- To utilize SciPy, you must first install NumPy as a requirement.
- The Intel distribution for Python improves the speed of common libraries and algorithms, especially data analytics, to yield better performance.
- Intel distribution for Python is an optimized Python version and certainly provides improved results than the stock Python version.
- After installation of the Intel distribution for Python, one should validate if the installation is effective and can be done with the command: python.

Further Reading

Python official website – https://www.python.org/
Awesome Python – https://github.com/vinta/awesome-python

13

ADDENDUM – REAL-TIME FUN EXERCISES WITH PYTHON

LEARNING OBJECTIVES

After reading through this chapter and watching the video lectures, readers shall gain knowledge on writing simple Python codes which shall enable the following:

- Finding an IP address
- Spell checker
- Internet speed checker
- Music player
- URL shortener with Python
- QR code generator.

Also, some more exercises are given for you to try yourself, but with a video tutorial link.

13.1 Introduction

This chapter is kept as the last one in the book for a reason. Readers are expected to use the knowledge they have gained throughout the book and to build some easy, meaningful solutions with Python. Every single problem statement provided in this chapter is very interesting and easy to try out. Video links for demonstration purposes are also provided for the readers' convenience. This will be a fun ride!

13.2 The Exercises – Try These Out

13.2.1 Find the IP Address of Your Machine with Python

The below piece of code snippet shown in Figure 13.1 can get the task done. The users must import the socket and use the method gethostname as shown. That is sufficient, the IP address of your particular machine will be presented as shown in Figure 13.2. Try this out; this is fun.

```
IP_Check.py - E:\DeskTop\PPTs for YouTube\Python\IP_Check.py (3.6.5)
File  Edit  Format  Run  Options  Window  Help
import socket as f
hostn = f.gethostname ()
Laptop = f.gethostbyname (hostn)
print (" IP Address for you " +  Laptop)
```

Figure 13.1 The code snippet for finding the IP address.

```
Python 3.6.5 Shell                                            –  □  ×
File  Edit  Shell  Debug  Options  Window  Help
Python 3.6.5 (v3.6.5:f59c0932b4, Mar 28 2018, 17:00:18) [MSC v.1900 64 bit (AMD6
4)] on win32
Type "copyright", "credits" or "license()" for more information.
>>>
=========== RESTART: E:\DeskTop\PPTs for YouTube\Python\IP_Check.py ==========
 IP Address for you 192.168.189.59
>>> |
```

Figure 13.2 The output – you got the IP address.

One can watch the demo through the video presented at the link:

https://www.youtube.com/watch?v=MvtDcQ g5edw

Hope you liked it. Let us get to the next one quickly.

13.2.2 Build a Spell Checker with Python

Using the Textblob, one can build a spell checker with Python. Importing textblob from Textblob has to be done as shown in Figure 13.3. Then, passing the sentence one wants to check for the spelling as argument is sufficient. Then calling correct() will correct the spell errors. That's it. Run the code and the output will appear

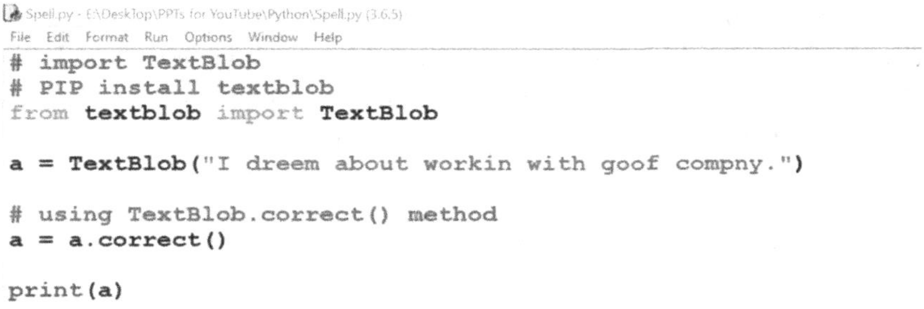

```
# import TextBlob
# PIP install textblob
from textblob import TextBlob

a = TextBlob("I dreem about workin with goof compny.")

# using TextBlob.correct() method
a = a.correct()

print(a)
```

Figure 13.3   Spell checker with Python.

without spelling errors. One can understand the way the code works through the results presented as Figure 13.4. Simple, try this out.

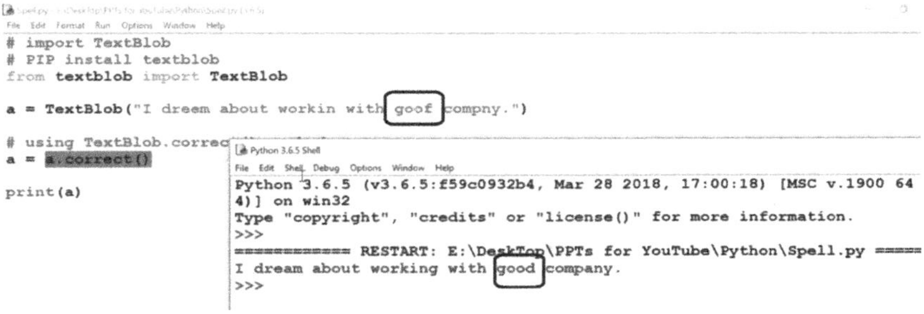

Figure 13.4   – The Spell checker and corrected spelling as output.

One can watch the demo through the video presented at the link:

https://www.youtube.com/watch?v=BnSXLcVY4TI

Can we go to the next one? The internet speed checker. Yes, you can check the speed of your internet connection with a simple piece of code.

13.2.3 Internet Speed Checker with Python

Well, the next one could be very useful for all of us. The internet speed checker. While there are many apps available to do this task, it would always be great for a techie to check this sort of things with their own code.

The code snippet is presented below as Figure 13.5 and it is very simple. One should import the speedtest library and use the methods download() and upload() as shown. That's it. When the same is run, one can get the data immediately as shown in Figure 13.6.

```
Speed.py - E:\DeskTop\PPTs for YouTube\Python\Speed.py (3.6.5)
File  Edit  Format  Run  Options  Window  Help
import speedtest
test = speedtest.Speedtest()
down=test.download()
upload=test.upload()
print(f"Download Speed: {down}")
print(f"Upload Speed: {upload}")
```

Figure 13.5   Internet speed checker with Python.

```
Speed.py - E:\DeskTop\PPTs for YouTube\Python\Speed.py (3.6.5)
File  Edit  Format  Run  Options  Window  Help
import speedtest
test = speedtest.Speedtest()
down=test.download()
upload=test.upload()
print(f"Downloa
print(f"Upload    Python 3.6.5 Shell
                  File  Edit  Shell  Debug  Options  Window  Help
                  Python 3.6.5 (v3.6.5:f59c0932b4, Mar 28 2018, 17:00:18) [MSC v.1900 64 bit (AMD6
                  4)] on win32
                  Type "copyright", "credits" or "license()" for more information.
                  >>>
                  ============ RESTART: E:\DeskTop\PPTs for YouTube\Python\Speed.py ============
                  Download Speed: 13338697.257562857
                  Upload Speed: 3318341.782845123
```

Figure 13.6   The upload and download speeds.

One can watch the demo through the video presented at the link:

https://www.youtube.com/watch?v=iBv3YOVapgc

Can we build a music player with Python, now? Yes, it's time.

13.2.4 Play Music with Python

Yes, it is possible. One can play music with Python. We have modules and libraries available to play music with Python. The below piece of code presented in Figure 13.7 can accomplish the task. There is a prerequisite to be met. The user must have done the pip install pygame. Also, the mixer must be imported from the pygame. That's it. The path for the music file must be included in the code as presented below. Then, one can call the methods, init(), load() and play(). Executing the code will play the music for you and it's music time!

```
# Here you go, we can play music with python!
# Do the pip install pygame, please.
from pygame import mixer
music = 'E:\DeskTop\PPTYT\Python\house_lo.mp3'
mixer.init()
mixer.music.load(music)
mixer.music.play()
```

Figure 13.7   Play music with Python.

You will receive the message on screen as shown in Figure 13.8 and then the music shall be played.

```
Python 3.6.5 (v3.6.5:f59c0932b4, Mar 28 2018, 17:00:18) [MSC v.1900 64 bit (A
4)] on win32                                                                I
Type "copyright", "credits" or "license()" for more information.
>>>
================= RESTART: E:\DeskTop\PPTYT\Python\music.py =================
pygame 2.0.1 (SDL 2.0.14, Python 3.6.5)
Hello from the pygame community. https://www.pygame.org/contribute.html
>>> |
```

Figure 13.8   Music with pygame.

One can watch the demo through the video presented at the link:

https://www.youtube.com/watch?v=zRMrvOnWZwA

Hope the readers enjoyed some good music through the last exercise. It is time to navigate to the next. Yes, we can get the URL shortener developed through Python. It's interesting.

13.2.5 URL Shortener

There are many websites available for us to get this task done. But, how about developing one? Yes, it is easy and nice to try this out. One can refer to the code presented as Figure 13.9 and can be tried to check how well it is working. The results are presented as Figure 13.9. As one can notice, pip install pyshorteners is a definite prerequisite. Then one should import the shorteners, as shown in the code snippet.

```
URLshort.py - E:\DeskTop\PPTYT\Python\URLshort.py (3.6.5)
File  Edit  Format  Run  Options  Window  Help
#URL Shorteners using python.
# It's simple!
# Do pip install pyshorteners
import pyshorteners as psn
url = "https://en.wikipedia.org/wiki/Sachin_Tendulkar"
u= psn.Shortener().tinyurl.short (url)
print (u)
```

Figure 13.9 URL shortener with Python.

Followed by that, the weblink which should be shortened is to be fed as an input into the methods as prescribed below. Simple, the URL will be shortened. One can refer the output screenshot (Figure 13.10) to understand the process.

```
Python 3.6.5 Shell
File  Edit  Shell  Debug  Options  Window  Help
Python 3.6.5 (v3.6.5:f59c0932b4, Mar 28 2018, 17:00:18) [MSC v.1900 64 bit (
4)] on win32
Type "copyright", "credits" or "license()" for more information.
>>>
================ RESTART: E:\DeskTop\PPTYT\Python\URLshort.py ==============
https://tinyurl.com/h3oxt8m
>>> |            I
```

Figure 13.10 Shortened URL.

One can watch the demo through the video presented at the link:

https://www.youtube.com/watch?v=bSlbRkL5UoU

13.2.6 QR Code Generator

It is time to generate some QR codes! Yes, Python can help you with this too. We can generate QR codes with ease. The prerequisites are getting these installed – pip install pyqrcode, pip install png and also pypng. Then, import the pyqrcode, png as shown below in Figure 13.11. Followed by then import QRCode from the pyqrcode. The string which you want to convert as QR code has to be sent to the method as shown in the code snippet (Figure 13.11). Also, mention the location in which you want the QR generated to be stored. One can see the results as presented in Figure 13.12.

```
# Here you go! QR Code with Python!
# Do the pip install pyqrcode without fail.
# Do the pip install png / pip install pypng
import pyqrcode
import png
from pyqrcode import QRCode
inpStr = "www.kt.ac.in"
qrc = pyqrcode.create (inpStr)
qrc.png('E:\DeskTop\PPTYT\Python\\QR.png', scale =6)
```

Figure 13.11   QR code generator with Python.

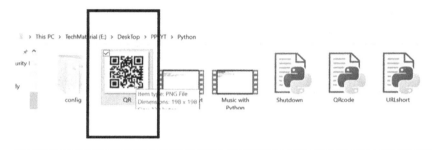

Figure 13.12   QR code generation.

Well, having seen some of the interesting exercises, we hope readers will also try out the following by referring to the video tutorials we present below. It will be definitely nice to try and we are sure that this will be a good way to complete the book.

- Speech to text conversion – https://www.youtube.com/watch?v=zEEAvOdTAqs
- Text to speech conversion – https://www.youtube.com/watch?v=HocZeknJEvk
- Language translator – https://www.youtube.com/watch?v=hnkxe9-_afg
- YouTube video downloader – https://www.youtube.com/watch?v=amHRwUEkCYQ
- Calendar with Python – https://www.youtube.com/watch?v=PctQyJ5WbAg
- Random number generation – https://www.youtube.com/watch?v=5B9aZ1T7oHU
- Emojis with Python – https://www.youtube.com/watch?v=fX53ie1AV2g

Key Points to Remember

- The entire chapter dealt with lot of practical exercises, and it is recommended to try these out.
- If errors do occur, it could be because of importing libraries and debugging can be done with that as a starting point.
- Learning these libraries/modules shall be very handy to build projects.

Further Reading

Python official website – https://www.python.org/
Awesome Python – https://github.com/vinta/awesome-python

Index

Pages in *italics* refer to figures.

Printed in the United States
by Baker & Taylor Publisher Services